INSIGHT INTO ADOPTION

ABOUT THE AUTHOR

Barbara Taylor Blomquist was born in Milwaukee, Wisconsin, attended Middlebury College in Vermont, and graduated with a B.S. in Sociology from the University of Wisconsin. She has conducted extensive research on teenage adoptees and currently counsels with adoptive parents. She is a past board member and Director of Volunteer Services at Epworth Children's Home in St. Louis where she created and conducted adoption groups. Currently, she serves as a board member, Vice President, Treasurer, and Adoption Consultant for Learning Consultants, Inc. in St. Louis and is their originator and coordinator of adoption groups for parents and adoptees. Barbara is married with three children, a daughter (biological), and two sons (both adopted). As is true for most writers, the author's thoughts and passions were created and developed by various experiences and events in her life. This is what has given her in-depth knowlege, understanding, compassion, and insight into the adoption world, especially regarding parenting issues.

INSIGHT INTO ADOPTION

What Adoptive Parents Need to Know About The
Fundamental Differences Between a Biological and
an Adopted Child–and Its Effect on Parenting

By

Barbara Taylor Blomquist

CHARLES C THOMAS • PUBLISHER, LTD.
Springfield • Illinois • U.S.A.

Published and Distributed Throughout the World by

CHARLES C THOMAS · PUBLISHER, LTD.
2600 South First Street
Springfield, Illinois 62704

ISBN 0-398-07201-9 (paper)

Library of Congress Catalog Card Number: 2001025705

With THOMAS BOOKS *careful attention is given to all details of manufacturing
and design. It is the Publisher's desire to present books that are satisfactory as to their
physical qualities and artistic possibilities and appropriate for their particular use.*
THOMAS BOOKS *will be true to those laws of quality that assure a good name
and good will.*

Printed in the United States of America
R-3-TH

Library of Congress Cataloging-in-Publication Data

Blomquist, Barbara Taylor.
   Insight into adoption : what adoptive parents need to know about
the fundamental differences between a biological and an adopted
child--and its effect on parenting / by Barbara Taylor Blomquist.
     p. cm.
   ISBN 0-398-07201-9 (paper)
   1. Adopted children--Psychology. 2. Adoption--Psychological
aspects. 3. Adoptive parents--Psychology. 4. Parent and child. 5.
Parenting. I. Title.

HV875 .B59 2001
362.73'4--dc21

                     2001025705

To my husband, Bob—for his loving support and enthusiasm. Without him, this book would not have been written.

To our children—Susan, David, and Jim—each of whom had a distinctly essential role in the creation of this book.

To all of the many adoptive families who in their own way contributed to the development and essence of <u>Insight Into Adoption.</u>

PROLOGUE

At the moment I am looking out my window at a beautiful scene—the day after a March ice storm. I see a sunny blue sky looking down on a rushing, brown, muddy creek. The evergreens, that yesterday were standing straight and tall, are now bent and slowly shedding their icy burden. Geese that only two days ago were noisily frolicking in a 60 degree spring day, are now gliding silently in icy water.

It is a picture of peace and beauty although there is evidence of past hardship. Yesterday I saw sleet, wind, ice, and cold. Today I see sun, melting snow, a quiet sense of relief. The physical evidence of yesterday's struggle makes today even more impressive because of the contrast. It is more moving than the average spring day we have been witnessing.

So it can be with people. Those who struggle and survive a personal storm can be strengthened by it. It is impressive to see.

The following work has been developing for years. It is only now when I am in the "day after" scene, that I can write about my struggle. My feelings and passion for my message are stronger now than when I was in the middle of my own personal storm with an adopted son. There is a calm in my daily life now, but there is still a churning in my emotions.

I feel strongly we all have a strength within us to be ourselves, to take the best within us and nurture it, letting it grow until it takes us over. We then can become what we are. It doesn't matter what our biological parents were, or were not. It doesn't matter if they gave us up for adoption. It doesn't diminish our value if they were struggling with insurmountable challenges. That fact has nothing whatever to do with the innate talents, abilities, and beauty found within each of us.

If I could transform the world, I would magically make every twelve year old see that he is special. I would cut all the negative ties to the past—someone gave me away, someone hurt me, or someone didn't love me. Those facts describe the adult taking those actions. Those facts have no bearing whatever on the value of the recipient of the acts.

Some adopted children experience an overwhelming journey in trying to establish themselves as worthy human beings. They can struggle for years with issues that are incomprehensible to the nonadopted person. My hope is the information contained within this work will apprise the nonadopted person, in particular, the adoptive parent, so he can look at the obstacles his adopted child may be facing. The parent may or may not agree with the reality of the obstacles, but I hope after reading the following pages, he will respect the fact that these issues are all too real for his child.

Then he, as a parent, can begin to understand his child's behavior. Only then can the parent's actions be motivated by enlightened understanding and resulting compassion. In this struggle, love alone is not enough. A parent must have the feeling of getting inside his child's head to feel the insecurity and fear and anger. Then, together, they can face the issues.

Many adoptive parents have been frustrated by working with counselors and psychiatrists who have had little or no personal experience with adoption issues. Some of these professionals give little credence to the deep and often camouflaged issues of their adopted clients. They may treat the symptoms and behavior without looking deeply into the root causes.

Because colleges and graduate schools of social work, counseling, and psychology offer little or no information on adoption issues, many adoptive parents have found the most valuable counsel has come from other adoptive parents or professionals with personal experience in the field of adoption. Necessity forces a parent to learn quickly, especially when the problem is hard to understand, and it's difficult to see any solution. Experience is invaluable.

Once the true source of the adopted child's pain is discovered, parents can reach the "ah, ha" moment we have all experienced. With understanding comes a new attitude and the impetus to change the whole atmosphere from negative to positive. The child and his parents will still have issues to deal with, but the source has been uncovered, and issues can be faced openly.

The goal of this book is to help parents comprehend the thinking process of their child, and to help social workers, teachers, and counselors approach their adopted clients in an enlightened way once they understand an adopted child has issues in his life unique to the adoptive process.

PURPOSE AND INTENT

In the more than 30 years I have been dealing with adoption issues, I have often been encouraged by adoptive families to put something in writing. It was felt that I had the advantage of "having been there." I have lived through the experience within my own family, have counseled adoptive parents for many years, and also spent 12 years working at a children's residential facility. The following pages are proof that I listened to these adoptive families and did put something in writing. This book is designed to flow as if I were talking with them.

Please understand there are millions of adoptees, but the problems addressed here apply only to a small percentage of adopted children who go through a difficult time assimilating their adoptive status into their lives. However, I feel the basic principles of adoptive parenting discussed here can and do apply to all adoptive families. Adoptive parents reading this book can gain a different insight into their child's reasoning, and this information can be used to avert some potential problems they might otherwise face. Professionals working with adopted children and adults rarely consider the "relinquishment" issues that their clients may be wrestling. Everyone touched by adoption can benefit from understanding the additional burden relinquishment and adoptive issues present for some people.

There is no startling information here (unless you have never delved into the adopted person's mind). Most people have not. Those of us who were raised by our biological parents have many things to learn from those people who were raised by adoptive parents. That is what this book is about.

Those of us who adopted children before the 1980s were handed a baby and told, "Make this child your own." It's no wonder some of us had problems. We were working on the premise of all nurture and giving no weight to nature. Many of us learned after years of frustration that nature will have its way.

The bottom line is that the more information adoptive parents have of the workings of their child's mind, the more harmonious their lives will be.

Younger generations can learn from the experiences of those of us who established adoptive families at a time when we were all kept in the dark. There is now so much more adoptive parents can do for and with their children. This by no means guarantees there will be no issues or problems to work through. It just means you as parents will know what you are doing. In this arena you will have an advantage over previous adoptive parents.

In this book you will find neither footnotes nor a bibliography. This is not meant to be a scholarly dissertation on adoption issues. There are many of those excellent books in the marketplace that should be required reading for all involved in the adoption field.

Instead, this work presents information and concepts that are generally known and accepted by all who are deeply involved with adoption issues. Unfortunately, for the most part, this does not include adoptive parents, nor many of the counselors they seek out in stressful times.

Most adoptive parents are given their child and rarely ever hear from the source again, whether it be an agency, a doctor or a lawyer. Adoptive parents set about living their lives believing their family will be just like all the others on their block. Sometimes it is.

This book includes all the issues that adoptive families should be told about. In years past, many families nurturing a "loss sensitive" child were completely in the dark as to the source of any problems. They felt they didn't cause them, and when their child exhibited troubled behavior, even he couldn't articulate the cause. Everyone was struggling with phantoms and phantom issues.

In recent years, light has been shed on those phantom issues, and from enlightenment came methods and solutions. Still, there are adoptions where parents are given no insight as to the additional issues they will be expected to handle.

The purpose of this book is to help fill that void. The information within is based primarily upon real life experiences relating equally to both sexes. However, in order to simplify the writing, I have used only the masculine pronoun throughout the book.

CRITICAL INFORMATION

The intent of this book is to provide realistic and factual insight into the world of adoption. It is possible, after reading this book, some people might come away with various negative thoughts and feelings regarding adoption.

It is not my intent in writing about adoption issues to project that image. Adoption is intended to be, and should be, a fulfilling, beautiful, rewarding, and enriching aspect in anyone's life. The following pages deal with some pitfalls not obvious to the unenlightened adoptive parent who was basically handed a child and told to "Make him your own." My goal is to help adoptive parents understand some potentially challenging factors so they can deal with them positively. This will enable them to appreciate the depth and breath of the "fullness of life" inherent within an adoptive family. There is an innate sense of loving abundance when you are touched by adoption and its uniquely wonderful children. All parties involved with adoption have the right to such an experience.

So, let's start our discussion, one-sided as it will be. . . .

CONTENTS

PART 3: COUNSELING HANDOUTS

INSIGHT INTO ADOPTION

Part 1

ADOPTION BASICS

Chapter 1

ADVICE FROM AN ADOPTEE'S PARENT

My husband and I have known many adoptive parents over the past 35 years. The majority had a beautiful experience in creating their adoptive family, while others had an extremely difficult time. I have great admiration for the adoptive parents we have known personally who were battered by the complicated aspects of adoption. They have gone through difficult years, but without exception, all have come through to a positive resolution, and their families are lovingly intact.

It would have been easier for us as adoptive parents had we known what was ahead of us. However, we were the generation which didn't anticipate problems. We didn't realize what our children were going through. Undoubtedly, we could have been of more help had we realized they were fighting "ghosts and demons" we couldn't see. We were told from the start not to anticipate problems, and we believed this with all our hearts.

Those of us who experienced problems loved our children blindly and could not see that their issues and resulting negative behavior came from a valid basis. We were, indeed, caught short. At the time, the only way we knew to help them was to keep loving them. Unfortunately, for the most part, they had to find their own way through the labyrinth of issues stemming out of separation from their birth parents (relinquishment). We had no problems with the adoption concept, and unfortunately, didn't understand the source of our children's problems. We could only stand by and catch them when they fell. We were frustrated because we didn't know how to help.

My fervent hope is that adoptive parents who read this work will be more enlightened than my generation of adoptive parents. This does not mean there will not be problems. Your child still may go through difficult times, but you will have the advantage of being able to understand their thought process. Whether you see the logic and sequence of their thinking or not, my hope is you will give credibility to their point of view. Your children can be fragile.

Long before I knew we would be an adoptive family I was intrigued by the concept. There seemed to be an exciting aura surrounding the process. Perhaps it is the unknown factor that makes adoption so mystical. It's hard to describe.

Adoptive parents face additional challenges, although most would agree the experience of creating an adoptive family is overwhelmingly positive. This work deals with some problem areas, and there is no question they can be very serious.

There are those overpowering moments when you look at your adopted child and are struck with the realization that he could have been placed in another family. Whether it be fate, circumstance, or divine intervention, that child you are hugging tightly is yours, and yours forever. Adoptive parents do not take their children for granted. These children are cherished indeed.

There is a deep satisfaction that accompanies adoptive parenting. The word "special" is overused when it comes to adopted children, but I sincerely feel adoptive parenting is special. In my mind, there is no question that adoptive parents give more to their children. Their emotions have the basis for a deeper foundation because everything they do is very consciously done. All becomes special because so much time and effort and emotion occur before the fact of the child's arrival. When the child finally arrives, it is indeed, a blessed event. Even though there may be some hard times, possibly even harder than with a biological child, it is still a blessed union.

I discovered an interesting fact while working at a residential facility for emotionally disturbed adolescents—20 percent to 25 percent of the children there had been adopted. Only 2.5 percent of the general population is adopted by a nonrelative, so their number was eight to ten times more than the adopted population in general. The environment there, with its disproportionate number of adopted children, only strengthened my realization that adoptive families have been overlooked and their unique issues have not been addressed by society. They have been alone for too long a time.

I hope information included in this work will show adoptive parents the inner workings of their child's mind. Many problems stemming from adoption are exacerbated because adoptive parents have never been adopted children. This is a place where most of us have never been. In our family we certainly had no clue as to how one of our two adopted sons was thinking.

We were motivated by love, while one of our sons was motivated by doubt and insecurity. It's no wonder we weren't on the same wave length .

Some couples feel apprehensive about adopting, and this is understandable. There are innate issues that can be troublesome. However, the feeling of taking an adopted child into your heart is so extraordinary that it is hard to describe to people who have not experienced it. We know we are fortunate to be among those who have.

We are grateful that life has blessed our family with both biological and adopted children. They have taught us different lessons. Adoption has taught us that love does not conquer all. Love is always present, but adoptive parents are forced to reach deep within themselves to discover their marvelous qualities of empathy, tenderness, tolerance, and compassion. Therein lies the blessing, the grace uniquely bestowed by adoption.

Chapter 2

INSIGHT

THE CONCEPT OF ADOPTION, like the concept of marriage, is a beautiful image. Life, with its twists and turns, can place people together in a cherished fashion. There can be a magical sense about an adopted child. Adoptive parents know their child is special, and beyond that, remarkable and extraordinary. Biological parents can say the same about their children, but for different reasons. Adoptive parents uniquely cherish their child for the simple reason that their child may not have been their child. Their child could very well be someone else's child, could be loved by another family, brought up in another household. They might never have known their child. This thought alone obliges the thinking process to deduct that the child is uniquely venerated.

Adoptive parents, like biological parents, love their children dearly and make many sacrifices for them. This love can blind some parents, indeed most parents, to the struggle innately positioned in some adopted children. Adoption is not seen as a problem for the parents, so they cannot fathom that it might be a problem for the child they love so dearly.

In the vast multitude of cases, the adopted child works through his issues successfully. It can take years but, unfortunately, the brunt of his battle seems to occur during the teen-age years, at a time when there is a multitude of other issues to face.

There are millions of adoptees who do not wage this battle. They slide right into their adoptive family and live happy, fulfilling lives. Only a small percentage of adopted children go through a difficult time assimilating their background information into their present entity. Our family, like many adoptive families, had one child who had a tough time and one child who had no problems at all. It is generally believed 15% of adoptees never truly get over the fact that the woman who gave birth to them actually gave them away. Even in adulthood, this fact can haunt them making it difficult for them to fully live life.

8

During adolescence, when a teenager is struggling to find out who he truly is, the adoption factor can be a roadblock. Most emerge into young adulthood with a healthy concept of themselves and incorporate their adopted status in a positive way. However, the adopted adolescent has thoughts and beliefs that the biological child has no reason to embrace. Since most adoptive parents were raised as biological children, these thoughts and ideas are foreign to them.

> The emphasis in this work is on the challenges an adopted child encounters in creating a healthy self-esteem if he cannot understand and successfully assimilate the facts of his relinquishment and subsequent adoption. *It is not intended as a place to look for problems where none exist.* It must be remembered that the vast majority of adoptive families usually face just the traditional child-raising problems and deal with them accordingly. In most cases, adoption is not a roadblock to healthy self-esteem. However, when an adolescent does struggle with this fact, it becomes, indeed, all too real an issue. It is not one to be discounted. In some cases, it can be devastating.

In introducing the reader to some common feelings and issues, it is hoped that parents will feel they are not alone, and all these feelings and issues are completely normal and logical for some adopted children. In most cases, a parent cannot change the course of this personal struggle for their child, but understanding the nature of the struggle should help all concerned.

When the adopted child doesn't truly comprehend what he is going through, it's natural for the loving parent to be baffled. The teen years are characteristically years of resistance to parents. This doesn't make the challenge easy for the adoptive parent who is dealing with these haunting relinquishment issues in their child. If the parent can make the journey easier for their child it would be wonderful.

However, in many cases, the adolescent has pulled away from his parents, so helping in an overt fashion is not feasible. Even in these cases, an understanding of their child's thinking process can be of infinite help to the parent. If the parent sees warning signs when their child is eight or ten or twelve years old, this may be the moment, when the door is still open, to embrace the issues in order to ease the journey. Verbal reassurance of inclusion and open communication can go a long way in helping.

However, I cannot emphasize enough:

DO NOT LOOK FOR PROBLEMS WHERE NONE EXIST!

Chapter 3

COMMON FEELINGS OF ADOPTED CHILDREN

THIS CHAPTER CONTAINS a list of some common feelings shared at one time or another by adopted children. It is simply a list of their feelings stated at a time when they felt safe enough to express them, usually in a group with other adopted children. No explanation is given here because the "logic" of their thinking is addressed elsewhere in this work.

Parents may find these statements difficult to read. They purposely are all listed together in random order. The effect is to give parents the idea of how all encompassing and pervasive these thoughts can be in the daily life of an unhappy adoptee. The ideas expressed are not comfortable for him, either. So, if you find these feelings disturbing and fatiguing to read, you will have gained a small sense of how an adopted child (and even some adults) may feel. The difference is he may feel this disquieting sensation daily. He never knows throughout his day just what will trigger a feeling. The reader can put the book down to escape these thoughts. The adopted child does not have that privilege.

Some of these thoughts will appear logical to the reader and some will appear illogical. However, they all can be disturbingly real and logical to the adopted child.

I feel ashamed that someone gave me away. I wonder if I am up to the standards of my new family. I wonder if I am a disappointment. Scott H., age 10

I feel I was a helpless pawn as a baby. People who didn't even know me made decisions for me. How did they know what was best for me? Marie S., age 12.

I was given up once by a set of parents, so it can happen again. My first set "loved me enough" to give me away. I wonder when my adoptive parents will "love me enough" to give me away. Jimmy N., age 11

10

Sometimes I feel life cheated me by taking something that belonged to me. I feel like I want to get back by taking from other people. Brian B., age 15

I feel I need to think about myself first. I need to take charge. People call me self-centered, but I feel I am the only person I can rely on. Others have left me. Mike A., age 15

I often feel like an outsider within my own family. When I ask questions sometimes they tell me that it's private information or that I'm too young to know. I wonder if I were their biological child if they'd tell me. Sarah R., age 11

I've read that some women who've been adopted are surprised when they get pregnant. Some even have dreams they give birth to an animal instead of a baby. I can understand this. We are made to feel less than human at times. After all, most people are born, but we were adopted. Angela N., age 17

I don't feel constrained by my parents' values. In the biological sense I'm not theirs, so I feel free to create myself. I can try out whatever I want. Their values don't need to be my values. Sam P., age 16

My parents say my mother gave me up because she couldn't raise me alone. I worry if one of my parents leaves or dies, if the other one will give me up. John H., age 9

Sometimes when I feel I don't belong, I want to run away and find a place where I do belong, where I'm comfortable. Marie P., age 14

I find it hard to trust people. Are my adoptive parents telling me all they know about my birth parents? Why are my birth records sealed? What are they hiding? Why so many secrets? I just don't trust people. Jack S., age14

I have a lot of fantasies about my biological parents. When I'm down, I think they must have been terrible people. My mother was probably a prostitute, and who knows what my father was. He's probably sitting in prison somewhere. At other times I fantasize my mother is a beautiful movie star and is searching for me because she loves me so much. Melanie B., age 13

I get very angry when I think my personal information is out there somewhere and I can't get my hands on it. It belongs to me. It tells me who I am. I need that information. Jason T., age 16

I often feel I'm just floating, not really tied to anything concrete. Maybe that's why possessions are so important to me. They are things that really do belong to me. I can touch them. Annie M., age 15

Sometimes I can't control my temper. I guess I'm mad at my birth parents and the system. I take it out on my adoptive parents. They're the ones who are here. Robert S., age 15

I don't even know my medical history. Everyone else does. For a long time I had terrible acne and thought it was because I was a bad person. I found out my birth mother had the same severe problem at age 21 when she had me. How much easier my high school years would have been if I'd known about the heredity factor. I thought it was the bad in me coming out. I didn't need to do that. Lee H., age 17

My adoptive parents are my parents and always will be. I've spent my life with them and I love them. I just hope they understand I need a part of my birth parents, too. I still may be the same person, but I'll feel more like I belong to the human race. I'll feel complete. Emily P., age 15

I wish I had the confidence of other kids. My parents or a teacher give me credit for something and it doesn't stick. I have so many doubts about myself. I don't believe them when they say I'm O.K. Thomas F., age 14

This list of quotes above makes for disturbing reading. One almost has the feeling that nothing will get through to the discouraged child to counteract these feelings. *These thoughts absolutely have to be refuted.* It may take years, and parents' and teachers' encouragement may fall on deaf ears for much of that time, but still encouragement and praise must be repeated over and over again. The child needs to hear that his value is not determined by the supposed value of his biological parentage. This will be addressed later in the book (see Chapter 18).

In dealing with adoptive parents, one hears constantly how tired they are of encouraging their child, while the child appears determined to prove himself valueless. At times like this it may be tempting to give up, but if the child has given up on himself it is all the more important that parents and teachers get more vocal in their praise. The behavior of the child sometimes defies praise, but ironically this is when he needs it the most. There is a popular saying that a child needs love most when he deserves it the least. That surely is true here.

Chapter 4

COMMON FEELINGS OF ADOPTIVE PARENTS

ADOPTIVE PARENTS' FEELINGS are rarely discussed. However, in a closed session with other adoptive parents there is the freedom to express some negative thoughts.

There appears to be safety in these sessions that is not felt with relatives and friends who have not gone through the same experience. Validity needs to be given to the emotions felt by parents of adopted children. Society usually tells these parents they are lucky to have these children, and they shouldn't complain. Being human, and sometimes fatigued, adoptive parents need affirmation that what they are feeling is understandable and acceptable.

THE EFFORT OF PARENTING—A feeling of *"We give more."* It is not uncommon for adoptive parents to give more to the parenting issues than biological parents. The adoptive parent thinks he is parenting a potentially deprived child who may just possibly not be their's to parent. This can cause adoptive parents to set up an overly protective environment. Often the thought of "this child could have been someone else's" can cause false competition (with ghosts of other parents). Adoptive parents feel the need, therefore, to be super parents. This can lead to burnout, particularly during their child's adolescence, when parents are doing more giving and getting little in return.

GOOD VERSUS BAD CHILD—A feeling of *"We got a bad one."* Due to some adopted children's insecurity within the family (at what point will they, too, give me away?), a child often tests the strength of his parents' love. Just how much bad behavior will they endure? The parents, naturally, are disappointed in bad behavior and may react in a rejecting manner. They, perhaps, had qualms taking on an "unknown" child with unknown heredity. At this juncture, it is understandable that the relationship can disintegrate.

The child reaffirms to himself he really is a "throw-away" child, and the adoptive parents think they did everything they could do, but heredity issues were too overpowering.

In reality, this testing behavior is a crucial time when the adolescent is asking through his behavior, "Do you really love me enough to put up with the bad in me as well as the good?" Parents need to express the *forevermoreness* of their family and prove they accept their child unconditionally. This is not always easy in the face of some pretty difficult situations. It is, however, absolutely essential in holding the family together.

It's common for biological parents to look at aggressive behavior in their child as merely being "a chip off the old block," and deal with it appropriately. In adoptive families aggressive behavior can prompt thoughts of "What do we have here? What are we in for?" There can be a normal tendency to overreact at this point.

PERMANENCE ISSUE—A feeling of *"Of course, this is forever."* When a family adopts a child, they know that he will be as permanent as a biological child. The relationship is forever. This is so obviously clear to adults that they don't discuss the fact with their child. They should.

This permanence is not always so clear and valid for the adopted child. As a child matures and conflicts develop, he may feel he is not performing up to the standards of his adoptive parents. Over a period of time, the child wonders just how much the parents will endure before they, too, give up and send him away. As preposterous as this may seem to parents, it is very real to some children. For this reason, it is imperative that parents, in good times and bad, verbally express the *forevermoreness* of the parent/child union. Bad times should not weaken the bonds. They are merely bad times to be worked through. If the adolescent gets this message, his need to test the relationship will be greatly lessened. He can relax with the knowledge he is secure within his family.

It's natural for an adopted child to question the strength of his parental bond when you consider he has already survived a broken parental bond. It is simple logic to deduct that any event that has occurred once, can occur again. Adoptive parents should not be threatened by this questioning. It only means the child needs to feel secure and grounded. Unfortunately, most of the time this questioning is not verbal, it is done with negative behavior which leads right into the old adage "A child needs love the most when he deserves it the least."

ADOPTIVE VERSUS BIOLOGICAL PARENTING—a feeling of *"It's the same, but it's different."* The only parenting role models most of us have are our own parents, who in the overwhelming majority of cases, were our biological parents. There is a difference in parenting, but most adoptive parents resist the fact there is a difference. There are teenage issues, as well as adoptive issues, facing the adopted adolescent all at the same time. It is the wise parent who recognizes this and seeks information and help if needed.

STRENGTH OF THE ADOPTIVE BOND—a feeling of *"Doesn't he like it here?"* When a child asks about his biological parents it can be disturbing for adoptive parents. If they feel their parenthood was tentative from the beginning, this questioning makes even more of an impact on them.

Adoptive parents should not feel threatened. Their child is merely inquiring about a part of himself that other children know about and he doesn't. It is a missing link he needs to complete his identity. This questioning is often misinterpreted by parents as a desire on the part of their child to find and perhaps live with his biological parents. In times of anger and distress, this could be the temporary motive, but in general, it's a healthy curiosity in his search for identity. When information is obtained, this confirms for the child he is now more like his friends. He, too, was born, in addition to being adopted. This fact serves as a grounding tool for him.

LOSS AND GUILT IN BEING CHILDLESS—a feeling of *"We resent it when the world keeps reminding us we are adoptive parents."* Adoptive parents are often told by adoption agencies their family will be just like all others. Adoptive parents want to believe this. In the beginning years when they are dealing with a young child, it is the same. Their child isn't old enough to comprehend the relinquishment concept. Around the age of six, seven, or eight he begins to understand. His world changes when he goes to school and studies heredity in biology class or his friends ask why he looks so different from his siblings and parents.

Adoptive parents are exposed to "You are so good to take in a child who isn't yours. He's very lucky to have you as parents. Do you know much about his background? Aren't you glad you never had to go through a pregnancy?" These and many similar comments remind adoptive parents over and over again their family is different, and others consider them less than real parents. Comments about these differences can be uncomfortable. Actually, a sense of being a family can be even more important to adoptive parents than to biological parents because there was a very real possibility they never would have had a family.

TENTATIVE PARENTING—a feeling of *"Am I or am I not a parent?"* Biological parents deal with a nine-month pregnancy. They know when it will end and when their baby will arrive. Adoptive parents don't have a definite time frame. Currently, the waiting period is very long, often years. After an adoptive couple has their child, they wait again for the court date to finalize the adoption. During all this tentative timing, it is only natural for parents to hold back a part of themselves just in case it doesn't work out. This can be emotionally trying putting the family in a lengthy, nerve-wracking state of flux. So much is beyond the control of parents. Deep down there can be an atmosphere of it all being artificial.

Once their child is part of the family, adoptive parents face decisions biological parents do not. A feeling of, "This is my child, but he isn't my flesh and blood," can bring doubts as to how strongly you impose your religion, morals, philosophy, and expectations.

There can be confusion as to whether to integrate the child wholly into the identity of your family or nurture the inherited traits the child may have. Differences between child and parents in an adoptive home often are suppressed because all involved want the family to be *real*, just like other families. This can lead to an unhealthy climate and closed communication.

At this point, ghosts may appear. Adoptive parents face the ghost of the biological son or daughter they never had, as well as the ghosts of the biological parents of their child, and other adoptive parents their child may have been placed with. The adopted child is dealing with ghosts of his biological parents, other adoptive parents he could have had, as well as feeling a competition with the ghosts of his adoptive parents' unborn biological children.

All these ghosts can set up a myriad of confused feelings. Parents can feel betrayed and resentful when their child makes life difficult for them. After their anger subsides, they feel guilty for embracing the thought, "Why are we going through this? He isn't even my child." This can lead to overcompensating behavior by adoptive parents and a sense they have to try harder. Overindulgence and permissiveness can follow.

Throughout the whole adoptive process, emotions may be submerged that later surface at unexpected moments. A newly adoptive mother in heating a bottle for her son their first morning was annoyed at his constant crying. She was doing her best to heat the bottle rapidly while his fussing continued. She looked at him and was shocked to hear herself say out loud, "Be quiet. Who do you think you are? You're not even mine." Fortunately, she was alone. She immediately felt overwhelming guilt. Her submerged anger at the whole adoption system came out in that one inappropriate statement. In stressful times, it's not unusual to say things that are not meant.

Adoptive parents go through a lot of wishing, wanting, and pretending all is well. Frustration is also present and should be faced honestly.

When problems arise, adoptive parents may be reluctant to share these issues with other family members. They may feel, and indeed be, more alone in their parenting if their extended family was hesitant or resistant to their adopting children. They want to avoid a possible, "I told you so" mentality. This only adds to their problems when they really need help and support during these times.

Adoptive parents have honest emotions. Society all too long has not been receptive to these feelings. Anger and frustration are often submerged by the thought, "I should feel lucky to have this child." Adoptive parents need to feel validated in their all too normal and natural feelings. This can be done within an understanding family atmosphere in an appropriate fashion or within support groups for adoptive parents. Above all, any feelings they have are honest. Adoptive parents have a different exposure to parenting than biological parents, and they deserve the acceptance and affirmation of those feelings which accompany their experience.

Chapter 5

LOGIC

BEFORE PRECEDING ANY FURTHER there is a bit of logic that must be stated. In order to work through any problems adopted children may be facing, I think this logic must be accepted in a realistic manner.

- Biological children are not adopted children.
- Adopted children are not biological children.
- There are differences between biological and adopted children.
- Therefore, there may be different issues in parenting them.

Adopted children are biological children only to their birth parents. Once they are relinquished and adopted, they are in another category. There are many areas of life where their position is different from what it would have been had they not been adopted. These differences are:

1. The biological child has two parents, the adopted child has four parents.
2. Usually, the adopted child does not live with any biologically related person.
3. The biological child belongs to his family through a natural process. The adopted child belongs to his family through a man-made, artificial process.
4. A biological child was kept by his original parents. An adopted child was not. (See the handout at the end of the book entitled *Factual Differences.*)

Chapter 6

FACTUAL DIFFERENCES BETWEEN BIOLOGICAL AND ADOPTED CHILDREN

THERE ARE, INDEED, factual differences between biological children and adopted children. Many involved in the adoption process wish these facts did not exist, but they do. In situations where the fact is disturbing to the adopted child, various issues can surface, often causing problems.

Below is a list of the factual differences and the ensuing issues that may arise:

FACT—*A biological child by nature belongs to his family. An adopted child knows he is not tied by blood and heredity to his parents and siblings. People somewhere matched him up with a family.*

RESULTING ISSUE—The arbitrary choice of adoptive parents can produce many thoughts and questions in the adopted child.

For instance:

1.   How permanent is this bond?
2.   What other choices (adoptive parents) were there?
3.   Were my parents the best choice?
4.   No wonder I feel like I don't fit. This isn't my family.
5.   Who are these people to tell me what to do with my life?

FACT—*A biological child sees physical verification of himself daily by looking at his family members. An adopted child never experiences this.*

RESULTING ISSUE—A biological child may have certain traits reinforced by the fact that his father is athletic and so is he, or his mother is a writer and he is good at writing, also. Aunt Mary may have been a genius at the piano and that ability comes naturally to him.

Often, when there are similar abilities or interests within a family, a feeling of belonging can develop, a feeling of, "this is who I am and this is where I belong." The adopted child yearns for this feeling, but his genetically inherited factors do not always produce a good fit within his adoptive family. He may lack the innate feeling that, like it or not, this is truly where he belongs because he is among his own kind.

The adopted child tries many things throughout his youth seeking what is comfortable. However, it is all virgin territory for him (and his adoptive parents). His natural talents and abilities may or may not fit into the life-style of his adoptive family. For instance, a quiet, scholarly child could be placed in a physically active family or vice versa. The self-image of the adopted child must be discovered one item at a time. There may be more trial and error as there is no script from which to read—for either the child or the parents.

FACT—*A biological child has one set of parents (one mother and one father). An adopted child will always have two mothers and two fathers.*

RESULTING ISSUE—The adopted adolescent child who feels he does not belong or fit into his adoptive family can question where he belongs. Who is he really? Is he more like his birth family and if he is, what are they like? This reasoning gives more latitude to experimentation in life, to go beyond the ground rules set up by his adoptive family. After all, they really aren't his original family. He often searches for a life where he thinks he should be, where his biological parents might be. He has more freedom to develop himself outside the guidelines of his adoptive family.

Sometimes, in drastic cases, as the child gets older, this quest for his denied identity can even lead to his leaving home. There are several theories regarding this phenomenon, but most think it is a search for one's roots, a symbolic search for a lost biological family. Often the adolescent will put himself in a lower socioeconomic life-style and slowly work himself up his *own* ladder. Perhaps, he doesn't feel comfortable being in a doctor's family or a carpenter's family, so goes out to discover his own level of comfort. This can be a painful journey and a very lonely one. He feels, however, he has no one to answer to but himself since he doesn't truly belong to anyone.

FACT—*A biological child belongs in his family by society's definition. An adopted child was placed by society into a family, but yearns for that natural connection.*

RESULTING ISSUE—When a child feels he doesn't truly belong to his adoptive family, he can go through a painful search for himself. Most young children want to be like their parents, and surely they want to fit into their family. Both the child and the parents look for common factors and emphasize them.

An adopted child is often more sensitive to being *in* or being *out*. During adolescence, he can go overboard in order to belong to a group, hoping to completely enmesh and lose himself in the identity of that group. This is a way to obtain an identity which he feels he lacks.

In families where there is an overlap of national heritage this can be used to create a common bond. In one family the adoptive father was Irish and English and the mother was of German heritage. The child was thought to be Irish and this was articulated throughout his youth as being *like Dad*. When this young man was in his 30s he confided to his mother, "You know, Mom, when I was young, I always wanted to be part German." In finding something in common, you may be excluding something or someone else. The adoptive mother was surprised to hear this and gratefully accepted the fact that her son, all along, wanted to be like her, also.

FACT—*The biological child was kept by his parents. The adopted child was "given away."*

RESULTING ISSUE—It can be difficult for adoptees to face and assimilate this rejection while trying to develop a positive self-image. Rejection is not easy for anyone to deal with. It is hard for others who do not have to assimilate a birth mother's rejection into their psyche to comprehend just how devastating this can be for some children.

A child between the ages of six and eight starts to understand the concept that he had to be relinquished before he could be adopted. The real impact of this abandonment usually hits a child around age eleven, just as he is approaching his adolescent years. At this point, the idea his mother gave him away can be overwhelming. Up until that age many nice adoption stories have set a happy mood for the child, but the facts and reality of his life can come together as he hits adolescence—all this at a time when he is trying to emerge as an independent, confident teenager.

At this point, a child can set up a self-fulfilling prophesy for failure. He can set up unrealistically high goals for himself and downplay any successes he may have. He is then confirming to himself that he is a loser. His low self-esteem feels very comfortable to him, and he can verify it by the fact he was given away.

Ironically, if a child can understand and accept his relinquishment by his biological parents, he can be released from the anger and belligerence he feels and displays toward himself and his adoptive parents. This is not an easy accomplishment for a teenager. However, if he can see his birth parents as people with both good and bad traits, he then can accept them and their actions, as well as himself, and his adoptive parents all in the same forgiving light. He must realize that the problems or issues faced by his biological parents have no relevance to his own self-worth. This is a quantum leap for a teenager, but one that, if successful, will allow him to proceed in a free-flowing acceptance of life, and he is then free to develop himself fully.

FACT–*Biological parents, dealing with biological children, do not deal with their child's feeling of abandonment. Adoptive parents may face this as an integral element in their child's self-image.*

RESULTING ISSUE–The adopted child fights many more demons in developing himself than a biological child does. When he is old enough, he understands the mechanics of adoption, i.e., one set of people went to another to have them decide where he should live and who his parents were to be. He was a helpless pawn in all this decision making, and he naturally wonders about all the other options, including the possibility he could have stayed with his birth parents.

One's search for identity involves incorporating your past heritage into your present life. However, the adoptee's true heritage has been taken from him. He can feel great anger at the system and hatred toward himself by assuming his past was negative. There are blanks in his life that biological children do not have. The fantasy facts the child uses to fill in the blanks are usually not positive; thus they do not contribute toward development of a healthy self-esteem.

The ghosts of all the people he may have become enter his mind at this time. It's difficult to feel grounded when you know you could have been a number of different people. A feeling of loss can impact the adopted teenager. He may feel that if he knew his biological parents, he would be more secure, because then he would know just who he really is. A mourning for his true lost self can be very real.

The sense of loss, in general, can be felt more intensely by an adopted person than by others because he is dealing with loss from his very beginning. He often is walking through life with a sense of hollowness, so when someone else leaves his life he may suffer more harshly. For example, a fifteen-year-old started a three-year bout with drugs when, within a month, his best friend moved a thousand miles away, his sister went away to college, and his beloved grandfather died. Three days after his grandfather's funeral this young man started to buy drugs at his high school. He sought drugs to temporarily stop the pain of his loss, of so many people leaving him all at once.

Another phenomenon created by the loss issue can occur when the adopted teenager "leaves the nest." Without a firm foundation of identity, this prospect can be more frightening than usual. The adopted child can threaten to leave or actually leave before society would deem it timely, thus saying to himself, "I'll abandon you before you abandon me."

Peer groups can become more essential for the adopted child than for the nonadopted child. If the adoptee feels he doesn't fit into his adoptive family, he may find a more comfortable identity within his peer group. He may feel more of a sense of belonging there. Sometimes, the feeling of trying to fit into a family that is so different can be exasperating. If he is the odd man out, this feeling can be partially negated when he is accepted into another group. If the child's feeling of self-worth is low, he may seek out a peer group where he is comfortable i.e., one with values below those of his adoptive family. He may feel this is the level he probably came from originally.

A growing child, adopted or biological, needs to feel acceptance. If he doesn't get it at home, he will look for it elsewhere. It is important that adoptive parents be sensitively aware of their child's potential feeling of being on the outside of their family. Parents may not agree with this feeling, but it can be painfully real for their child.

When he is not given certain delicate family information or included in decisions or activities, he may interpret the cause to be that he is not a full-fledged family member. Great sensitivity and awareness should be practiced during these times. You are dealing with a child's reality, not the adult's reality. What is right and what is true doesn't matter when your child is coming from another point of view. This can be quite challenging when the thinking process of the adopted child comes from such a defensive position. You must get inside his head and determine how he is feeling.

Awareness of his feelings and open communication can go a long way in averting problems. Dismissing his attitude as not reasonable or as a passing phase is only counterproductive. Everyone has had the feeling of being on the outside of a group, of not truly being accepted. Imagine then, a budding adolescent in this intensified position. It is only natural the child may interpret some statements or actions in a negative way although that was not the intent of the parent.

FACT—*A biological child has an undeniable right to be in his family. An adopted child lives with the fact he was adopted into a family, not born into it.*

RESULTING ISSUE—As a child matures and finds he is different from most other children, he often faces social stigma, embarrassment, and a feeling of being isolated from others. He can feel cheated in life because his *real* parents were taken from him. This sense of being cheated is compensated for, in some cases, by the child stealing, thinking things are owed to him. He thinks taking from others is a way of getting back at a world which took something from him. He feels he has taken back some control of his life and is no longer helpless.

The heritage and traditions of the adoptive family become his traditions, but are they really his? When an adoptee inherits a clock from his grandmother, does it really have meaning? The clock is real but the fact that his grandmother is part of his heritage may not feel so real.

Religion, philosophy, and beliefs of the adoptive family may or may not coincide with the religion, philosophy, and beliefs he would have been exposed to if still in his birth family. They had their own generations of tradition.

The ugly duckling syndrome can have fertile ground for flourishing in the adopted child's mind. There are many life-styles and many types of families. In most families, a child is raised to believe his family has the best approach. An adopted child, upon reaching an age where he questions the values of his family, has the added aspect of "I wonder what the values of my other family might have been?"

When an adopted adolescent does not feel he fits into his adoptive family, he can develop resentment toward his parents whom he feels are trying to make him into a Johnson or Jones or Schwartz. He knows he really isn't, and anger and resentment can flare up into an attitude of "Who do you think you are, trying to make me one of you?" He can resent having to live a life which he thinks is a lie.

FACT—*The adopted child needs more questions answered than the biological child who has the security of still being with the family he was born into.*

RESULTING ISSUE—Once the adopted child realizes he could have been in a number of families, he needs answers as to why he was placed in his present family. His role in the adopted family, in his biological family, and his role in the grand aspect of life may be questioned. Honest communication with the adopted child should answer his questions. The child needs reassurance, strong and constant reassurance.

He can have very valid fears about his heredity. One young adopted adult was horrified when he saw the picture of a serial killer in the newspaper and noticed the remarkable physical resemblance he had to the man. The serial killer had been born in the same city as the adoptee, and the young man realized they could be related to each other. Circumstances like this can occur in an adoptee's life.

It's natural for a child or a person to question his biological past. There is a natural curiosity. Once given honest answers in a loving way, a child is able to plug those facts into his identity chain and build on them. The child needs to be assured all along the way that it is he who is the important person, and it is *he* who needs to develop all the potential he has.

Building blocks from both of his families may or may not be key ones for him, but they are there nonetheless, for him to accept or reject. He should be allowed to choose and develop his identity incorporating the parts of his past with which he feels comfortable.

Chapter 7

WHY IS MY JOB SO DIFFERENT?

PARENTING IS NOT EASY for anyone. It is an ongoing process where parents face issues in a time and environment different from their own childhood. Adoptive parents have all the normal issues that parents face daily, but they also have many more. Many subjects must be dealt with differently in families where a child is adopted.

So far we have been talking about these differences from the child's point of view. When you put all these differences together in one package and place that bundle in a home, one can see what some adoptive parents experience.

These differences (discussed in detail elsewhere in the book) are listed below:

1. An adoptive parent can feel more responsibility to make life happy for their child. After all, were he placed in another family, there is a hypothetical possibility he would have preferred life there. Adoptive parents struggle with phantom parents, all the other possible adoptive parents their child could have had. A strange aura of competition can develop with these phantom people.

2. Adoptive parents may have a child who thinks they, too, will some day abandon him. Erratic testing behavior can result from this attitude and parents are forced to deal with it.

3. Adoptive parents may be living with an adolescent who is having a hard time fitting into his adoptive family. They may hear, "Who do you think you are to tell me what to do? You're not my parents!" He is actually asking the question, "Are you my parents?"

4. Adoptive parents are dealing with, in most cases, a largely unknown genetic history of their child. There is always the question of how much to

nurture and accept their child's innate genetic make-up and how to assimilate these differences into their family structure.

5. Adoptive parents live with the fact they are one of two sets of parents in their child's life. Their child needs to think of both sets in a positive light in order to develop into a healthy person. It is the job of adoptive parents to create this atmosphere.

6. Adoptive parents live in a world where other parents may not view them as having different issues. An adoptive parent realizes his is a more complicated job, but feels uncomfortable in acknowledging this. He tries to slide into parenting in the same manner as his friends and neighbors.

7. Adoptive parents have a tendency to be super parents. Since they may not have been able to conceive a biological child, now that they're parents, they feel the self-inflicted pressure to do an extraordinary job. Great disappointment can follow when these parents think extraordinary parenting should be followed by extraordinary gratitude.

8. Adoptive parenting can start out on a tentative basis. First, they did not produce a child, then a time span (often years) wondering if they will ever get a child, followed by a wait for finalization in court. In order to protect themselves, adoptive parents may have a tendency to hold back in their emotional commitment just in case it doesn't work out.

9. Adoptive parents are reminded in many ways that they are not the biological parents of their child. Friends and family make many comments ranging from, "Aren't you lucky to have gotten a child," to "I'd never put up with all his problems. I'd send him back."

10. Adoptive parents often don't have any role models since they were raised by biological parents.

11. In our society adoptive parents must go through a process of proving to strangers (agency, legal personnel, etc.) that they will make good parents. This can be difficult when a couple is dealing with their childless state. Biological parents don't need to prove their prowess at parenting before giving birth to their children.

12. Adoptive parents have a tendency to compare their success as parents with biological parents. This is an apples and oranges comparison. Adoptive families have more and different issues throughout the years.

13. Adoptive parents may be living and parenting with a difference in the acceptance factor. Sometimes, an adoptive father is dealing with the male heir issue and passing on his name to a child who is not genetically the same as he.

14. Adoptive parents may unknowingly be creating an atmosphere whereby the child thinks one parent wanted to adopt him and the other was reluc-

tant. This can happen when one parent appears to be more distant emotionally or when job demands keep a parent away. Some children may take this personally, thinking one parent really doesn't accept him as their child. He may become defensive.

15. Adoptive parents may be living with a child who feels his place in the family could be temporary. Because adoptive families lack blood ties, verbal reassurance that their child will always be theirs is necessary. This fact is implicit in biological families.

16. Adoptive parents may be raising a child who exhibits more extreme behavior than a biological child. The adoptee may think his family's boundaries are not *his* boundaries because he is an artificial member, so he has freedom to experiment.

17. Adoptive parents and biological parents lead similar lives when children are very young, but adoptive parents can feel sad as they see their child grow up and develop into someone who has little similarity to them. They have spent years trying to make their family homogeneous.

18. Adoptive parents may tend to "over control" their child. The tie that binds them at times doesn't feel as strong as a biological tie might be. There can be an inclination to control in a surface manner with the hope that all will stay in place.

19. Adoptive parents may live with a child who is sensitive to being included or excluded in family matters. A biological child, by definition, belongs.

20. Adoptive parents may be forced to face some deep judgmental issues, some of them racial. An adoptive parent may have to deal with accepting a child with different genetic qualities than their own biological child would have. Helping their adopted child incorporate a healthy image of his biological parents forces adoptive parents into acceptance of these same people.

21. Adoptive parents are privileged to be part of a system where a child is born to one set of parents and embraced by another. The many forces involved in ultimately determining the placement and ensuing identity of a child are great. This at times appears to be as much of a miracle as the creation of a child's life. The question, "How did this particular child end up being ours?" is a question no biological parent ever ponders.

22. Adoptive parents do not see the physical verification of themselves in their children. In biological families physical similarities are discussed and can be grounding and comforting. The adoptive family does not experience this.

In summary, many of the differences appear to be challenging. Once parents can empathize with and understand the thinking process of their child, these differences can be readily handled. In some cases, the differences can be a strengthening bond within the family.

The adoptive family has a grounding and verification of humanity as a whole. Identifying characteristics within one's own family are missing, but if a healthy attitude is taken, parents can look at their child as a blank piece of paper where everything is possible. They look for clues as to what may be. They do not feel boxed in by their own family limitations.

This can be an exhilarating experience for both parent and child. To nurture what there is to nurture without preconceived ideas about what is logical can be a wonderfully freeing experience. In an open-minded, healthy, adoptive family this can be reality, their philosophy for living their lives. What a joy this can be for both parent and child.

Chapter 8

TASK OF DEVELOPING A SENSE OF SELF

I feel different from other kids. I feel they're in the main-stream, and I'm on the outside. They know where they came from, so it's easy for them to know where they're going. They can focus better than I can. I feel like I'm just floating around.

Don P., age 14.

THE TASK OF GROWING UP can be quite different for an adopted child. It is important to point out the additional issues he faces.

Developing Self-Identity

An adopted child comes into a family with a large part of his true identity obscured. He is expected to assume the identity of his new family. Facts from his biological past can help anchor him into the world, but he is denied this in most cases. During adolescence, if he doesn't feel a kinship with his adoptive family, he will embrace his peer group in an exaggerated manner making it more of an identifying factor. He needs to belong somewhere, and feeling he doesn't belong to his family, uses the peer group instead.

An adopted child's sense of self can be vague, and he may feel more lee-way for experimentation. He doesn't necessarily feel bound by his adoptive family and may fantasize about the life-style of his biological parents. He may indulge in what he thinks is his biological parents' style and make it his own. Such a child usually assumes he comes from a low socioeconomic status, seeks such a group, and then develops contacts where he thinks he might belong.

The adopted adolescent has several selves with which to contend. There is the person he fantasizes he would be were he still with his birth family, as

30

well as the self he might be if he had been adopted by other people. This opens up many avenues of choice for the imaginative child. He also, of course, is in constant competition with the nonexistent biological child his adoptive parents might have had. All these imagined beings can prompt many questions about who he is and who he should be. Playacting for his adoptive parents can be a factor if a child thinks he must submerge his real person to become the person his adoptive parents want for a child.

If an adolescent feels he doesn't belong in his adoptive family, an "ugly duckling" syndrome can ensue. The more he feels excluded and the more he senses he is not compatible with his family, the more difficulty he has in establishing his sense of identity. His identity and true feelings may not be bad, but the fact that he senses he doesn't fit in may cause him to think he is wrong, and the rest of his family is right.

He may feel he has to please in order to be accepted. Anger and stress can develop from this situation. It is generally believed that in order to develop a healthy sense of self, your historical and traditional issues need to be factored into your image. In this area the adopted child is blank. He can be told facts about his original heritage, but he will never experience their influence. They have been amputated from his life.

Labels often tell us who we are. When we are very young, we are told we are good, bad, smart, dumb, talented, awkward, average, etc. We act out roles as if in a play. We are a son, daughter, student, artist, athlete, and many more. Sometimes it can feel safe to fall back on our prescribed sense of identity. We can regress to being our parent's child or the little brother or the big sister. However, it doesn't always work this way for the adopted child. During adolescent years, if the adopted child feels he doesn't truly belong to his family, he doesn't have this identity crutch to fall back on. He has been told he is a Hamilton, a Jones, or a Schumacher, however, he knows deep down inside that he really isn't because he doesn't feel it. Instead, he feels a sense of loss, of being very alone, separate from his family. To some adopted children labels are artificial boundaries because they feel they don't belong within their family, hence their family's boundaries don't apply to them.

There is a positive side. If a child can fully accept the relinquishment by his biological parents and see them as human beings with human traits, he is then free to create himself in his own way. He may see the labels of his adoptive family as artificial when applied to him. Great freedom can be enjoyed and used by a young budding adult to find his own way, without the usual constraints and family expectations he may not want to embrace.

In a healthy adoptive family, all of the positive factors in a child's past should be introduced to him. There are two sets of parents and two sets of traditional and historical factors that will always be a part of the child. Often, when a child is adopted, his biological past is kept from him, however, it is always a part of his life and who he is.

A Tenuous Existence

Sadly, an adopted child may feel that since one set of parents already gave him up, the adoptive set may also. He may not sense unconditional love and acceptance in his home. He may try to role-play what he thinks his adoptive parents want in their child. This may or may not be who he truly believes himself to be. He may be submerging his real self so he can *be* their child and fit into the family. Usually, adoptive parents are not aware of this because they are raising their adopted child as they would a biological child. The corrections and training along the way are natural to parents, but an adopted child can interpret these required adjustments in behavior as necessary to become accepted into the family.

A child needs to belong. This is essential for him to feel secure. He looks for similarities with other family members. He definitely wants to belong to this group. Unfortunately, he can be overly sensitive to being excluded from his family. Again, this is not something parents are aware of because in their minds their child will be theirs forever. The slightest exclusion in making a decision or being excluded from a family activity can be misinterpreted by a child as caused by his not being a full-fledged family member.

In trying so hard to act like a true family member, a child may suppress some of his honest emotions and feelings, sensing that within his family they are not appropriate. As an adult, the adopted person may still repress his feelings. In future adult relationships, holding back his emotions by only showing his good side, can be an impediment to a healthy partnership.

Developing Self-Esteem

It is easier for a child to develop a healthy self-esteem if he knows he emerges from good people and hence, must be good himself. Children identify with their parents. If a child perceives he comes from inadequate parents (who couldn't take care of him), it's natural for him to incorporate inadequacy into his self-image. The child can feel humiliated by the fact he is the offspring of parents who couldn't care for him.

Adoptive parents must perceive birth parents as people who were facing issues they could not handle at the time of their child's birth. They were neither good nor bad people, just people facing pressures and making a decision that adoption was the best option for their child. If adoptive parents can truly be accepting and understanding of their child's birth parents, this attitude can be imparted to their child. This allows their child to positively integrate both sets of parents into his self-image.

The Child's Reality Versus Real Reality

An adopted child's perception of himself can be very confusing and may seem illogical. The lack of logic is not important. Reality is not important. What is imperative is that the child is dealing with what *he* perceives to be real. This is what parents must understand.

Getting inside their child's head and facing his issues (real or imagined) is how a parent can be most beneficial. Many issues have no logical basis for existing, but in the child's mind they are not only logical, they are very real and applicable. Sadly, an adopted child fights many demons that exist only in his head. A parent should not dismiss these demons in hopes their child will outgrow them. The child's innate feelings of rejection and abandonment provide fertile ground for many problems, and these issues must be faced.

An adopted child may be more inquisitive about his existence because his birth circumstances are different. He may become distrustful and difficult to deal with because so many facts of his life are kept secret. Parents at this point need to be very approachable and willing to discuss issues bothering their child. Through open and honest communication they can attack these demons with logic and love. The issues should never be discounted.

A "killing off" of the ghosts their child faces is a good place to start. It is difficult to take on ghosts. They need to be faced and dealt with so they can be put aside, allowing both child and parent the freedom to deal with the realities of day-to-day living and loving. If the burden of what might have been can be shed, people can turn their attention to the present reality. This is a healthy place to start in convincing their child he is forevermore a part of his family and is unconditionally accepted and loved.

Chapter 9

THE IMPACT OF LOSS

I struggle with relationships. I have this empty feeling they won't last. I think everyone will leave me eventually. When a friendship ends I take it as one more person giving up on me. I feel like there's an empty hole inside me that will never be filled.

Phyllis R., age 16.

S O FAR, WE HAVE BEEN talking about adoption issues. However, adoption issues are really loss issues. A baby or child cannot be adopted until after he or she has lost his or her first set of parents. That, by definition, makes adoptive parents the second set of parents.

The awareness and impact of this loss differs with each adopted child. Some are keenly aware they are in a "substitute" family, while others slide right into their adoptive family as if it was the most natural, comfortable, perfect place to be. It's hard to determine why children react so differently. If adoptive parents are dealing with a child who feels he is in a substitute family and is angry about it, many problems can arise. These issues are discussed elsewhere in this work. In this chapter, I would like to take the reader through the feelings that a "loss sensitive child" may experience.

All people have experienced loss. However, surely one of the most powerful losses is that of a child losing his parents. Even though we may not have experienced that traumatic event, we can empathize with the adopted child if we look back upon our own experience with loss. As small children we may lose a relative or a close friend. A loss of schoolmates and friends and comfortable surroundings can occur in a move to a new neighborhood or new town. During adolescence there were the lost girlfriends or boyfriends. Remember never wanting to date someone who was on the rebound?

Is the adopted child on the rebound? He lost his parents at a very young age when he was not able to cognitively handle his loss, and subsequently could not grieve. Problems that occur during childhood could relate back to that loss. Often adoptive parents speak of an anger in their child and are in a quandary as to its cause. Anger, however, is one of the stages in the grieving process.

Not being very developed and aware at the time of their relinquishment, the adopted child cannot grieve at the time of his loss, but may grieve throughout his childhood. This difficult behavior often seems to come from nowhere, so parents don't know how to handle it. The cause eludes them and understandably so.

When adults lose a friend through a move or another circumstance, or lose a relative through death, they feel sad. The impact is felt immediately— and they grieve immediately in some way or other. The adopted child cannot grieve immediately at the time of his loss.

An adoptee is reminded of his different status many times throughout his childhood, but most particularly when he is an adolescent and is striving to discover just who he is. He is keenly aware that he does not have firm footing underneath him. That sturdy grounding was removed by the adoption process.

The child may have extremely loving and understanding parents, but their power and influence over him stop at the genetic door. Neither they nor their child truly knows the genetic makeup with which they are dealing. This lack of information can impact the struggling teenager seeking to fit into life. Frustration and anger are common feelings at this point. They appear in many antisocial ways, but the bottom line is a feeling of anger over his initial loss of identity.

In the days of closed or traditional adoptions, parents were given little or no information about their child's biological parents. The attitude at the time was nurture will be more important than nature.

Years later, we know this to be untrue. Both are factors in a child's life. In past years, there wasn't much conversation about adoption because there wasn't much to say. How much better it would have been had adoptive parents been given birth parent information and told to help their child grieve for his first set of parents.

Psychologists tell us we need to grieve in order to move on with our lives. Sadly, many adoptees are stuck in the anger stage of grieving and don't realize the source of their problem.

Life has told them for years they were fortunate to be raised in a wonderful, loving family. What more could they want? They surely shouldn't complain because they were undoubtedly better off in their adoptive family than with their biological family. The child was made to feel guilty when he yearned for his first family.

Throughout his childhood he knew something didn't feel right, but he wasn't guided to a resolution of his feelings. He wasn't allowed to move through all the stages of grief and emerge on the other side able to establish a healthy relationship with his adoptive parents.

Obviously, some adoptees who are not as sensitive to loss as others don't struggle with this "sourceless anger." They fare just fine. On the other hand, studies have shown many adoptees struggle with personal relationships throughout their lives, even though they don't show outward anger or resentment. Some fear rejection so they don't date or marry. They may have a hard time launching a job search, finding it easier to stay in a substandard job because there they won't be rejected.

A 34 year-old woman, Phyllis, had difficulty sticking to a planned wedding date. She had been dating her fiancé for seven years, and each time a wedding date was set she found some reason to cancel it. In hearing Phyllis speak, one could sense her unresolved anger. She was visibly agitated when talking about her birth mother and said she would never want to meet her because of her intense hatred. Phyllis couldn't understand why her fiancé was still around. She said to him, "How dare you love me, how *dare* you love me! I'm unlovable. My mother gave me away."

A 35 year-old man, Jack, in a discussion with his adoptive mother said, "But, Mom, my mother gave me away!" He leaned forward in his chair and repeated the sentence *emphasizing* each word slowly and deliberately, "My mother   gave   me   away!" Even though Jack had been told his family adoption story and heard the word adoption his whole life, he still looked upon the concept as inconceivable.

Phyllis and Jack did not go through the grieving process for their lost birth parents nor for their lost original identity. They are stuck in their anger which keeps getting in the way of having healthy, trusting relationships. Both Phyllis and Jack need to grieve so that their anger dissipates. At the end of the grieving process a peaceful acceptance occurs. Neither Phyllis nor Jack has found that peace.

Many loving, wonderful adoptive parents are stymied as to why their child is so difficult to deal with. Temper tantrums and resistance seem to be the norm.

Children need to feel it is O.K. to talk about their loss. They need permission to feel sad. They need to accept their relinquishment and loss as part of their life. Then they can move on and accept their adoption.

In these and other similar cases, if adoptive parents or counselors can see the unresolved anger for what it is, they may be able to guide the person back to their sense of loss so they can go through the grieving process. After many years of harboring this anger, it can be extremely hard for the adoptee to face it alone. It has become a comfortable, although unhealthy companion.

Adopted children can experience much denial. A protective wall (no one will ever get close to hurt me again) can become thick and rigid over the years. If a hole can be pierced through their protective covering, the walled-up, childlike feelings of primal loss for their birth parents and natural heritage can spill out. Once labeled, the denial can be addressed, and the adoptee can begin to heal.

Those who are not adopted will never know the depth and breadth of this initial, primal loss. We can remember the devastation of losing a boyfriend or girlfriend during our teenage years and the feeling our world has ended. If we lost a close relative through death, we can remember that feeling of loss. In all of these cases there was a loss, a grieving period, and a moving on with life.

In the case of relinquishment, the adopted child's loss can be ongoing and grieving may never begin. In most cases, a phantom set of parents was lost. Usually, firsthand knowledge of them is unknown. The imagination of the adopted child swings from their mother being a beautiful movie star (on their good days) to a streetwalker or prostitute (on their insecure days). It is hard to grieve for a person when you know they are an essential part of you, but you don't know what to grieve about.

Adopted children are reminded of their adopted status when they learn about their friends' birth. Charting a family tree in biology class again reminds the fourth grader he is different from his classmates.

In adolescence, when teenagers embrace the parts of their parents they like and reject what they don't like, adoptees realize they don't have two parents like their friends, but they have four parents. Do they reject the movie star or the prostitute? How can they reject a phantom when they can only imagine their characteristics, and those characteristics keep changing depending upon a mood or sense of self? Frustration is a natural result. Adolescence is hard enough without this additional burden.

It is often awkward for adoptive parents to talk about adoption with their children. Parents are caught in making difficult decisions. If they talk too much about adoption are they reminding their child he was not born into the family, and they view him differently because of this? Are they telling him this is a subject they think about? There is a divisive factor in bringing up the subject as opposed to living a life just like all the other households on the street and not talking about it.

On the other hand, relinquishment and loss are part of the child's life. He must face it, again and again. If the child is comfortable enough to talk about his loss he will have an easier time working through the grief process, no matter what form it takes. It does not always need to be antisocial and overt. But, one cannot deny the child has lost a set of parents. The loss is real.

The answer probably lies in walking a very fine line. When a child is vulnerable or sad and needs consoling, adoptive parents can be very helpful in guiding him through his feelings. Children can't understand many of these concepts. Adoptees over and over again talk about the "black hole" inside themselves. As children they did not realize why it was there.

Many studies have proved conclusively that newborns know their birth mothers. They will react to stimuli from their birth mothers and not react to others. It is hard to explain, but it is a fact of nature. A baby taken from its birth mother does not have conscious knowledge of this act. The breach occurs on a much, much deeper level. Some adults have a hard time fathoming this even though numerous studies prove it.

We must guide adoptive children having problems with anger in moving through their grief. Even though intellectually they might understand why their birth mothers didn't keep them, emotionally they may have a very hard time. The children know they would never "give away" a baby, so how could their birth mother give them away. They need to accept the sadness, and in ideal cases, move from sadness to understanding to acceptance and forgiveness. This is a lot to ask of a child and it's no easy task.

Chapter 10

TROUBLED BEHAVIOR PATTERNS

When I'm feeling really mad, I show my worst part to my
parents. I need to see if they love me when I'm bad as well
as when I'm good. I guess I'm testing their love.
Danny S. , age 11.

LIFE WITH ANY CHILD would be easier if they would verbalize how they feel. Unfortunately, children are often reluctant to talk about issues and, instead, act out how they are feeling. It is natural for adults to react to the behavior and not look underneath for the causes. A child's negative behavior is often followed by negative consequences from parents or teachers, and then the child feels even worse. He still has his problem that caused his negative behavior and, in addition, adults are now down on him, as well.

In previous chapters we discussed issues adopted children face. In this chapter we'll discuss the resulting behavior patterns. If parents can see beyond bad behavior (and that's not always easy), they can deal with both the behavior and its cause.

Testing Behavior

Sometimes, an adopted child will test his adoptive parents and others in his life to see at what point they, too, will give up on him. Because he was abandoned once, the child is convinced he could be given away again. He will test the other person's patience and limits by acting in a negative manner (often the way he thinks his biological parents act) to see just how much he is loved. Later in life, this same person can do his testing by being overly demanding, making it difficult to maintain a healthy, long-term relationship. This sets up a self-fulfilling prophecy of failure.

Behaving as Fantasy Birth Parents Behave

If an adopted child thinks of his biological beginnings as negative, he may want to be just like those phantom parents and act out in a way he assumes them to be. This can involve sexual promiscuity since he believes he was the result of such activity.

There are many ways a child can connect his behavior with the perceived behavior of his birth parents. He can abuse himself with drugs and alcohol; he can find friends in a lower socioeconomic environment where he believes he belongs; or he can set unrealistically high, unattainable goals so he will always fail. These behaviors then verify his own negative self-image.

Expressing Anger

Adopted children experience many of the normal teenage issues, but in addition, adoptive families deal with many other issues unique to adoption. A despondent teenage adoptee can feel anger toward his birth parents for abandoning him, the system for putting him where he is, his adoptive parents for making him live a life where he doesn't fit, and himself for being inadequate. If his self-hatred is strong enough, a child's self-destructive behavior can be a release for him. Drugs and alcohol can dull his pain. A child's anger is often directed at his adoptive parents just because they are there. They make convenient targets for unloading frustration and anger.

At the end of this book there is a section including handouts used in counseling support adoption groups. One is titled "Handling your Angry Child" and can be read for further information.

Exhibiting Lack of Confidence

The adopted child lives with holes in his past, and all too often, fills up those holes with imagined negative "facts." A lack of confidence can be manifested in many ways; self-destructive behavior, lack of trust in people, self-fulfilling prophecy of failure, attacking values of others when he feels inadequate in upholding them, lack of planning for any future (he has no past, thus no launching pad), and many more. His fear of bad heredity can block him from moving forward with his life.

Stealing from Life

The adopted child can rationalize that something was taken from him (his birth parents), so it is only fair that he take from others. This can take the form of stealing tangible items. He somehow thinks he deserves to have these things.

A feeling of hollowness and emptiness can haunt a child who feels he is missing something. If he has this sensation, it's difficult for him to give of himself. He may become more of a taker in life than a giver. Giving and loving may be hard.

Patterns Inconsistent with Adoptive Family

Many studies prove how strong heredity can be in all of us. Temperament, talents, and abilities can be inherited factors.

Even though a child is removed from his biological environment, he takes genetic qualities along with him to his new family. His innate temperament may or may not fit into his adoptive family's life-style. He may be an emotional person surrounded by a staid, emotionally controlled family. He may be an intellectual, quiet child in an active, social family. All sorts of combinations may develop which may not be conducive to a harmonious match.

Numbing the Pain

Drug use is prevalent in our society. Many young people believe the mistaken notion that using drugs or alcohol will numb their pain and make their problems go away.

The question of "Who am I?" takes on a different aspect when one has been transplanted from one family to another. While under the influence of drugs, the user's sense of reality changes. In some instances, the adoptee can see reality is not a firm thing because he has the power to change his reality by using drugs.

He is aware that the reality of who he is was changed for him by other people when he was a baby. If his reality can be manipulated by other people or by himself through the use of drugs, it may occur to him he may have power over his reality while not using drugs. This concept that he may have control over his life can be startling to him. Up until this point he felt he was a pawn of others who determined his family and his destiny.

Experimenting Freely

If an adopted adolescent takes the attitude he is not living with his *real* family, he then can logically conclude that their values do not extend to him.

He can be free of their value system and constraints. This, coupled with the thought that his genetic predisposition was more negative than positive, frees the child to engage in activities that his family would think taboo. He thinks he is different anyway, so why not live a different life-style?

An adopted child may not feel tied down by a preconceived or predetermined identity. This openness to extreme groups can be an exploration hoping to find a sense of belonging and a comfort zone with his chosen group. He yearns to be completely enmeshed, thus gaining some identity. This can come as quite a surprise to adoptive parents who have thought all along their child belonged to them. The child can search for an identity far outside the family's set of behavior criteria.

Fear of Another Rejection

In contrast to the above experimenting mode, other adopted children who are afraid of being abandoned one more time (this time by their adoptive parents) play, instead, the role of the perfect child. They hold their emotions back and are afraid of causing problems. They try very hard to fit in. This is sometimes accomplished at the cost of keeping their true selves submerged.

This suppression of real thoughts and emotions can develop into a habit and a false front to hide behind throughout life. An adopted child may not trust people enough to show them his true self. He shows them what he thinks they expect so his relationship with them will last. Obviously, in future adult relationships this can cause problems.

Living with an Exaggerated Sensitivity to Loss

This issue can be paramount in an adopted child's life. It appears to be subtle, but it can be explosive, making a great impact throughout the child's development.

A young adopted baby or child starts life having already experienced loss. Studies have shown a fetus becomes accustomed to its mother's heart beat and the rhythm of her life. A newborn baby is comforted by being held close to its mother and feeling the same sensations it did in the womb. It is said even the mother's voice is comforting to a newborn because the baby has heard it for months.

Now, if you remove a baby from this comforting position, it becomes clear there is a reaction even though the baby cannot verbalize or understand. There is a "feeling" of comfort being no longer available. Surroundings and people are new and unfamiliar, and adopted adults often speak of this mystical feeling. They say they remember as babies the different ways they were touched and held. Many adopted teens talk about sensing a lack of stability during their babyhood.

Jane, now 29, was adopted through a Catholic adoption agency at a time when it was the custom to baptize babies when they were just a few days or a few weeks old. Jane says, almost as if she remembers and can still feel the loss, "On such an important occasion as my baptism, there was no one there who loved me. Only the social worker and the priest were there." When Jane makes this statement, one can sense this episode in her life still affects her. A happy occasion for most people brings up sad, empty feelings for Jane.

As life progresses, an adopted child may feel loss more keenly than a biological child when a playmate moves away or a relative dies. The feeling that no relationship lasts forever is reinforced. It is as if the adopted person has a healed scar that is opened again and again. The adoptee's sense of aloneness can be very intense in these circumstances.

In addition, trust becomes an issue. Lack of a sense of trust leads to a sense of insecurity, and the child may feel he can't trust anyone to stay in his life. Everyone wrestles with this at some point, but those who are adopted may not feel as secure in their placement in this world. They can be knocked further from a centered position each time someone leaves, and may have a harder and harder battle getting back to a balanced point each time. Adoptive parents, who are not aware of this loss issue, may think their child is overreacting to situations. They may make him feel childish when their child is really in need of emotional reinforcement in the form of reassurance that people special to him will stay in his life.

Another aspect of this sense of loss may occur when a teen approaches the years when his friends are getting ready to leave home to go out on their own. The adoptee also wants this, but in doing so is inflicting another loss upon himself. If the teen is not secure in his identity, this may be a more difficult transition than it is for his friends.

To compensate for this inadequate feeling, the child may leave his family in an explosive fashion rather than in a relatively smooth way. He may cause great discord between himself and his parents. This makes him feel justified in leaving. He may find himself attacking what his family is and what they stand for. He then can leave them with greater ease, thinking they are having problems anyway, and it's better to be off on his own.

Leaving Home

If this attitude mentioned before is taken to its farthest point, the teenager may literally leave his family home at a younger age than is usually considered normal. He may drop out of high school to begin a search for where he thinks he truly belongs. He can feel empty and go looking for people and activities to fill that emptiness.

He often thinks he has to start at the bottom because he has no history, no heritage. He puts himself in the gutter of life and slowly climbs up a ladder of his own making until he finds his comfort zone. He may realize he doesn't belong in the gutter, so he gets a job or more education. He may still think he is capable of more, so accomplishes more. Once he has achieved some goals, he feels he finally has an identity and knows he accomplished it all by himself.

This can be a very strong place for him to be, even though he attained it in a very difficult fashion. He is, after all, looking for stability and a secure place in the world. He knows who he is not, and he feels all alone in his search for who he is. Independently, he has found his own identity separate from both his biological and his adoptive parents. Many mistakes and wrong turns can be made along this path in the search for his physical and psychological roots.

This is extreme behavior and is not common, but it does happen.

Part 2

WORKABLE SOLUTIONS

Up until now we have been discussing some heavy issues that may appear to be hopeless to newly adoptive parents. However, the vast majority of adoptions are successful. The saying in the real estate business is that the three most important considerations in buying are "location, location, location." In the adoption arena, the three most important considerations are "identity, identity, identity."

Adoptive parents may know their child as wonderful, exceptional, and loved. The best part is that he is theirs. This is all well and good for parents, but does their child know this? Unless he is told and shown how his parents feel, he may not believe it.

Ironically, just as I was about to begin editing this section I received a phone call from a very dear friend in another state. We have known each other for over 30 years, and both our families have adopted children. Mary called to tell me her elderly mother had passed on. We talked for a half hour, and after hanging up many of her thoughts stayed with me.

One thought that overshadowed all others was the statement, "My mother truly loved me. She often said the best thing she ever did in her life was give birth to me." Mary said she and her mother used to have a repartee whereby the daughter would say, "I love you powerful, Mom." Her mother would reply, "I love you fierce, Mary." How blessed my friend is, for no person nor situation will ever take the power of that love away from her.

Adopted children may be fiercely and deeply loved by others, but they will always know their first mother did not keep them. The strong love necessary to give up your child so he may have a healthier, safer, better life is lost on a young child. They can go through years of wondering why they were not kept by their birth mother. Those of us who have worked with adopted children often hear, "If they had loved me enough they would have found a way to keep me."

Adoptive parents can do everything right and still have problems with their children. It is not uncommon for adopted children within the same family to have varied reactions to their original relinquishment. In the Jenson family, one son, unhappy at home, left at age 16 to live a questionable life roaming from city to city, sometimes getting into trouble with the law. His accomplished older brother often said, "I got a spectacular deal. Growing up I've seen many families, and I never saw one as great as my own. My family is wonderful, and I am what I am because of them." Two boys raised by the same parents saw their circumstances through different eyes. Parents need to surround their children with a positive and loving atmosphere, but they still may have a child who is so angry at life and his birthparents that he cannot appreciate and absorb his adoptive family's love.

The following chapters are focused toward letting your child know he is loved. We need to remember we know it, but he may doubt it. We have to tell our adopted children over and over again how precious they are—even when they are trying to prove otherwise. Their behavior which may be shouting, "I am bad," often is really asking us, "Am I bad?" We need to be steadily ready with positive answers.

Adopted children deserve and need a strong identity developed by themselves and their loving families. They are not born into a warm, fuzzy nest-like environment. They all are removed from their original source, and those of us involved in their lives need to convince the doubters among them that the nest they are put into is one of support, acceptance, appreciation, and of course—fierce love.

So, let us now proceed to see what we can do.

Chapter 11

LACK OF ADOPTION CONVERSATION?

I feel a part of this family as long as I do what they want. I feel I don't fit, but I have to do a good acting job to conform to the family. I don't feel real.

Patsy M., age 15

Just because your child doesn't talk about adoption, don't for a minute think he doesn't think about it—probably more than you could imagine.
When asked, your child might say being adopted doesn't bother him, but you would be surprised at studies that show adoption is a definite issue in his life.

THE FACT THAT OUR ADOPTED CHILDREN don't talk with us very much about their adoption is a very misleading factor. There are many reasons why they don't want to discuss it. They think it is a separating factor and not a uniting one. They think parents may feel awkward discussing it, talking about it brings up the fact that there are differences in the family, and it reminds them they were artificially included in the family.

Adoptive parents say over and over, "Oh, my child doesn't care he's adopted. He never discusses it." The fact that your child doesn't want to discuss it does not mean it is not an issue with him. It just means he does not want to talk about it.

Studies show that adopted children are aware of their adoption on a daily basis. This is not bad; it is just a fact. Adoptive parents don't think much about the adoptive aspect of their relationship because their love for their child has nothing whatever to do with the fact that a child is adopted or biological. Because it is not a factor with parents, they erroneously think it is not a factor with their child.

Adoptive parents say and do things daily that have a subtle way of distancing an adopted child. For instance, when twelve-year-old George asked his father how much money his father made, the father's response was "That's not appropriate information for a twelve year old to have." That response was good and honest, but George walked away thinking that if he were a biological son, his father would have told him what his salary was. George's father at this time never thought of the adoption factor, but his son did. George talked about this incident for the first time when he was 32 years old—twenty years after that conversation. It obviously had an impact on him.

Because adoption is not an issue with a parent or grandparent, the conclusion that it is not an issue for the child may be very harmful. In this case, a simple added sentence such as, "No twelve-year-old should have this information," might have helped.

We cannot always protect our children from life's reminders that they are not our biological children. Eight-year-old Linda was found crying in her room one day after a visit from their next door neighbor, Suzanne. Linda's mother went to comfort her and asked, "What's the matter?" During Suzanne's visit most of the conversation centered on the remarkable resemblance Suzanne had with her two-year-old daughter. The hair color, eye color, and facial features were all mentioned as being identical. Suzanne exhibited great joy in the fact she had produced a daughter who resembled her so closely. Linda answered her mother's question through her tears saying, "I don't look like you. I don't look like anybody."

Adopted children are going to have these and similar experiences throughout their lives. This is just one aspect of adoption that adoptees need to accept. There are differences in biological and adoptive families.

It is important not to become obsessed with the adoptive status of the child, however a sensitivity to his adoptive status is healthy. Any conversations about heredity, inherited personality traits or physical traits, or background roots will obviously remind the adopted child that he is not included biologically within his family. This makes him a biological outsider. This is not important to his adoptive family, but don't assume it is not important to him. Awareness and empathy are essential.

Chapter 12

INCLUSIVE/EXCLUSIVE

I desperately want to belong to my adoptive family. I want to fit in. I'm always looking for similarities between them and me. I want there to be common ground.
Kevin A., age 13

> **Inclusive words and activities should be stressed in an adoptive family. Because inclusion or exclusion is not a factor in the parents' feelings, they are not aware of the many times they may unwittingly remind their child he is adopted.**

THE FACT THAT WE ARE tall or short, have blue or brown eyes, are adopted or biological are merely facts we live with. They are neither positive nor negative, but we are reminded of these things now and again. When we see a 250 pound football player on television, we perceive him to be large and that makes us aware we are not large. When we cannot reach an item on the top shelf in the grocery store, we are reminded we are short. When we notice someone who has blue eyes and is wearing a blue sweater, we are aware we have brown eyes. These things are not inherently bad or good, it's just that daily life regularly reminds us of our features.

The adopted child is reminded he is adopted when he sees a strong physical resemblance between two people or when he hears conversations about a child having a relative's nose, mouth, eyes, sense of humor, or when he hears the phrase "chip off the old block." He is reminded when he sees a pregnant woman or a childbirth scene in a movie. He is reminded on a continual basis.

There are many ways that a child becomes aware that his adoptive status is different from most of his friends. The more he is reminded, the harder it is for him to "belong." He can run across this daily. People who have never been adopted are surprised that there are continual reminders in our society.

Because the adoptive status is not a daily issue with adoptive parents, they often unwittingly make statements that remind their child he is adopted. When this is brought to the parents' attention, they are very surprised. It was not on their mind at all. They merely said something in a normal fashion. Here is where crawling inside the adopted child's head can help. If we look at these statements from their child's point of view, we might not make them.

A currently popular method of "time out" is used by many parents when their child is misbehaving. This message to the child is exclusive and not inclusive. Sending a child to his room or isolating him from the family is often done. The message is, "We don't want you with us until your behavior is proper." An adopted child hears the message, "When I misbehave, I am sent away from the family. I can stay with the family only if I am good. If I misbehave badly, just how far away will I be sent?"

This is not logical to nonadopted people, but if we crawl inside the head of an adopted child who has (in his mind) already been sent away from his birth parents, we can understand his thinking process. With adopted children discipline methods that do not isolate the child from his family may be more effective. This is a good opportunity to let the child know that no matter what happens, the family will always be together. Nothing, not even his bad behavior, can tear apart the family. This gives the child the security of knowing he will always belong.

> It is not healthy to always "walk on eggshells" so as not to hurt the adopted child, but a little sensitivity and awareness can go a long way in making the adopted child feel included instead of excluded. Getting inside the child's head and looking at life through his eyes can be very helpful.

An ongoing complaint of adoptive parents is their child's need for constant reassurance. This "over and over again" need can be exhausting for parents. It's helpful to remember that the tie that binds the adopted child to the family is not the same tie the biological child has. There are many times in the life of an adopted child that he doubts himself. He needs to hear again and again that he is accepted, appreciated, and loved by family members.

Parents may not feel the need to say it, but adopted children feel the need to hear it. Parents know the relationship with their adopted child is as strong, if not stronger, than with a biological child. Adopted children don't know this. They often need to hear this message when their behavior is at its worst. This is when they doubt themselves the most.

In a family having problems, the child and the parents are in pain. The difference is that the parents are adults and should be able to understand the source of pain. It is helpful if parents at this juncture can separate the child from the behavior and realize their child is sending a message that he hurts. Find out how he is feeling. Get inside his head, be empathetic, and reassure the child.

Good children behave badly at times. Separate the behavior and the child. Deal with the bad behavior as an item and how the child is feeling as an item. Learn to be a good interpreter of behavior. It's easier for children to communicate through behavior than through words. This presents a puzzle for parents until they can learn to see behavior as a symptom of what their child is going through.

Chapter 13

NOT ONE AND THE SAME

At times I wonder what I would be like if my birth parents had kept me or if some other family had adopted me. I wonder if my adoptive parents ever compare me to a child they might have had, but never did.

Patty F., age 12

Your love will never turn your adopted child into your biological child.

OUR ADOPTED CHILDREN are adopted children and our biological children are biological children. They are not the same. There is a difference. When this is acknowledged there is then a freedom to help the adopted child develop, grow and soar to his own individual heights, free from preconceived ideas.

In years past, much energy was spent by adoptive parents trying to make their adopted child into a biological child. Much of this is still going on.

One of the saddest cases of this was a family I dealt with who finally gave up on their son , Clay, at the age of 22 because, "he was too different from the rest of our family." Instead of identifying and nurturing their son's talents and gifts, the parents, in essence, told Clay what his talents should be. The parents' ideas didn't fit in with nature's ideas. There was frustration and sadness that didn't need to be there.

About this time, Clay found part of his biological family and went to live with them. His adoptive family said he fit in with them better anyway. What an opportunity that adoptive family missed—a lifetime of appreciating their son for the individual he was.

An adopted child arrives in our home with so much to offer the world. His gifts and talents are there to be explored and nurtured. Because there is no biological heritage shared with his parents, it's realistic to say it may take some exploration to find where his abilities lie.

For instance, to use an obvious example, a large muscular athletic man probably will have a son who looks similar in build. The father expects that his son will be athletic. The biological son may or may not be, but the probability is there.

In the case of an adopted child there are so many avenues open that are outside the realm of the adoptive family. It is this very fact that can add to the child's feeling he does not "belong" to his family. This fact, also, is instrumental in the adopted child wondering who he is. He knows he does not copy the inherited traits of his adoptive family, but what family does he copy? It may take a lot of experimentation to find the answer.

When a young adoptee does explore avenues he might be interested in, he may feel alone. He may not have the family history to make him feel secure in developing talents of a musician, athlete, or scholar. He thinks he may be walking down a dead end path that won't materialize after all. He feels he is only experimenting—and indeed he is. He has no sense of history to guide him.

With a lot of emphasis on genetics, the adopted child may erroneously believe he inherits his biological parents' tendency to use drugs or alcohol, or be sexually promiscuous. Even though genetics does have some influence, there should be a healthy emphasis on the control each of us has over our own lives and the development of our own interests and talents. Inherited talent is nice, but hard work, dedication, and a passionate interest can take a person far. The individual and unique nature of every human being is what should be emphasized.

Chapter 14

POSITIVE TERMS AND DESCRIPTIONS

I often feel alone, abandoned. Was I that worthless that someone would give me away?
Jacob G. , age 13

Always speak of your adopted child's biological background in positive terms.

IT IS NOT UNREALISTIC for an adopted child to believe he came from a negative and troubled background. He was, in fact, removed from his natural background. That in itself proves to him it was not good.

In a child's mind, the next logical thought is that if he did come from a negative situation, he then also, is negative. That is his heritage. This becomes very simple logic—false, but simple.

Some adopted children spend years *testing* their adoptive parents. Fortunately, this is a small percentage of adopted children, but if you have a child in this small percentage you can experience years of heartache. These parents keep loving and supporting their child while their child's negative behavior intensifies. Often, the parents have no idea why their child is behaving in such a destructive way.

This type of child thinks, "My biological parents gave me away because I was bad, how bad do I have to be before my adoptive parents give me away?" Of course, adoptive parents are not thinking of giving away their child. Again, this is not in their realm of thought or possibility, and they are not aware it is in the mind of their child. The child's tests escalate and his behavior can spiral downward even though his parents keep loving him. The child is certain that if his behavior gets bad enough he will be thrown out.

In one case a young man, Scott, left home at the age of 16 to live in the inner city in another state. He felt he didn't *fit* into his adoptive family who lived in the suburbs. It's not unusual for someone like Scott, with this mental stand, to go where he feels he does belong i.e., a few rungs down the social ladder. What often happens is the person finds he doesn't *fit* there either. He pulls himself up a notch or two and finds he still doesn't *fit*. He keeps improving his situation until he finds a comfort zone. Then he knows who he is because that's where he is comfortable. He has, in fact, found his own level in society determined by himself and his experiences, not determined by either his adoptive or biological families.

Scott returned home for a visit at Christmas time when he was 18 years old. Things were still a little tense and awkward. He was in the kitchen with his mother having a conversation, and all of a sudden Scott stopped talking while the proverbial light bulb went off in his head. His mother looked at him, saw the expression on his face, and asked if he was all right. Scott looked at his mother and said, "There was love here all the time and I couldn't see it because of my anger." Obviously, hugs and tears followed. A lot was revealed in that sentence.

It is crucial that an adopted child be told about his natural background and heritage. It's important that he knows he was taken away because of prevailing problems present at the time of his birth. This does not mean he came from a *bad* background. It means his biological family at that time could not handle the problems facing them, knew the child could be vulnerable, and wanted their child raised in a healthy, positive, loving, safe environment.

Most adopted children upon hearing this think that if their biological parents had loved them enough they would have found a way to keep them. For them, this is a normal, logical line of thinking. It's hard for any child to accept there could be any reason or cause ominous enough to cause a child's separation from his family.

Adoptive parents can only repeat and emphasize that their child's welfare was the overwhelming factor for the biological parents to make an adoption plan. All parents want the best for their children, and the adopted child is no exception. His biological parents were looking for a healthy, loving environment so their child would have more advantages than they felt they could provide at the time of relinquishment.

The nobility and sacrifice of relinquishment is understandably hard for a child to comprehend, but adoptive parents, through positive words and attitudes toward biological parents, can help their child develop a positive self-image, knowing he came from good, not bad people. This should be an ongoing learning experience so the child feels good about himself.

Some adoptive parents know devastatingly negative facts about their child's biological background. If this is the case, it's important to explain how a harsh childhood can cause some people to do bad things. Under other circumstances the child's biological mother or father may have behaved in a more socially acceptable manner. This emphasizes even more why the troubled parent didn't want their child to have the same life they had.

There is really never any reason not to find goodness in a child's biological family. Most people do the best they can. Good people sometimes do what we believe to be bad things. It is all too easy to judge from afar.

Chapter 15

PARENTS ARE MIRRORS

I don't think my parents think I'm very good. It seems they expect me to mess up my life. They don't give me the benefit of the doubt. They don't have high hopes for me.
                                                            Jennifer A., age 12

A child looks to his parents as to a mirror to see just who he is. What does your child see when he looks into your eyes? Does he see approval or criticism, acceptance or judgment? Does he see love?

As a young child develops and understands that he is not in his biological family, it is obvious he begins to wonder why he is different. Since a child's world is egocentric, it is again obvious that he thinks he must have been the problem for someone to have given him up for adoption. In his mind he was given away. Nonadopted people cannot imagine the enormity of that concept.

The next logical phase is to wonder what it is about himself that is bad. In his mind, if he were good, he would not have been given away. Some adoptive parents have negative expectations of their child when they know the biological parents were using drugs, alcohol, or were mentally ill. When this is the case, they may be looking for such signs in their child. Any expression of this "expectation," as subtle as parents may think it is, may be just the excuse their child is looking for to act out in a way he imagined his biological parents might have.

Adoptive parents need to be vigilant about their thoughts and expectations. A child will readily pick up on these. If they feel their parents don't trust them to do the right thing, they may feel they are indeed bad, and may act accordingly. A constant sensitivity to words and deeds is necessary. High expectations will get better results than low expectations.

Approval and acceptance and unconditional love are so important to a young growing child. We all mirror our thoughts in our faces as well as in our words. Think of the message you are giving your child while interacting with him. Is your attitude helping your child to grow or is it making him feel worthless and inferior? When you realize that your child may already be feeling inferior to other children because he was (in his mind) given away, you can see the importance the parent's demeanor plays.

Parents must keep asking themselves, "What message does my child receive when he looks into my face? How do I interact with him? What kind of a mirror am I? Does he feel better after interacting with me? What image am I reflecting back to him? How do I make him feel about himself? What does he see in me as his mirror?"

Chapter 16

HOPES AND DREAMS—REAL OR FANCIFUL

I wonder who I truly am. I wonder who I would be in another family?

Phillip F., age 13

Who is this child under my roof? What do I expect of him?

Parents' expectations are perhaps one of the greatest areas of variance between biological families and adopted families. Although adoptive parenting is for the most part more challenging, this is one area where it can be easier than biological parenting.

Many adoptive families don't see this as a gift. They have a child without the perimeters their biological child would have had. Even when some facts are known about the background and gene pool their adopted child came from, there are always areas that they don't know. An adopted child comes into a family with a much cleaner slate than our own flesh and blood.

When a biological child is born, the family immediately sees someone's nose, hands, eyes, etc. If a little boy has his baseball-playing uncle's physique, we often assume he will take after that uncle. After all, if his uncle was a success, there is no reason for the boy to quit just because he doesn't like baseball.

Parents have a natural tendency to push their biological offspring into roles that they already see within their family tree. They put physical and mental limits and expectations on their child who might try to be something or do something that has never been done in their family. Parents may feel it is not in the genes and therefore, discourage their child from wasting his time in a futile effort (in the parent's mind).

Now imagine you have a child and you don't know his limitations. What a gift! If that little boy doesn't like baseball, you think O.K., let's explore something else he may like and be good at. Adoptive parents have sketchy ideas about the biological and mental limits, but there is always the unknown factor. Maybe there is some musical or artistic or athletic talent in their child's background that was not mentioned at the time of adoption. It is worth exploring, always a possibility.

The tragedy occurs when an adoptive family tries to mold their adopted child into the person they believe their biological child would have been. Sometimes this may work, but often there is a lot of frustration on the part of the parents and the child. The parents are disappointed in their child, and the child knows it. Even though the child may have strong talents in other areas, he may pursue the areas chosen by his parents so as not to let them down.

Conversely, if the adoptive parents look upon their child as a gift, as all children are, they can embrace the opportunity to work with nature in exploring and developing their child's potential. They have values and standards of course, but the child can be viewed as a blank slate.

Many areas can be pursued. Nothing is beyond the realm of possibility. What a way to look at parenting! All parents should approach their children with this attitude, but when you have a biological line going back several generations, you have a tendency to limit your child to your known family perimeters. With an adopted child, parents needn't be haunted by family limitations or expectations.

When one family adopted Joshua, they were told he had great intellectual potential. This was not a particularly intellectual family although they had a great respect for education. They didn't push Josh, but he always seemed to do very well in school and loved school. He ended up with a straight A average throughout his schooling and finished his formal education with a Ph.D.

Years later his adoptive mother was looking through Josh's old records and was surprised to read that both his biological parents were B and C students. She had forgotten this part of his record, but she had always remembered the statement the adoption worker made that their son could have outstanding intellectual potential. Was it the family's assumption that Josh would do so well? Was it their subtle expectations? Would Josh have gotten a Ph.D. if raised by his biological parents? These questions are never answered, only asked. It does make one wonder.

It is so important for adoptive parents to question again and again just what their expectations are for their child. Are they selfish expectations?

Are they adopting a child for their own fulfillment? If parents can get themselves and their egos out of the way, it enables them to work freely with their child in exploring his potential.

Here is where it is easier than with a biological child. If parents can go forth with an open mind and not set expectations as to what talents their child should develop, they have the freedom to explore it all. They can look at his potential with wonder and questioning, unfettered by family history.

It is also essential the adoptive family accept their child with all the potential he may bring with him. He may have gifts and propensities that are very different from everyone else in the adoptive family. Unfortunately, in some families, these differences are not readily accepted. Before an adoption ever takes place, adoptive parents should do some soul-searching to determine if they can willingly and eagerly accept differences.

In all fairness to the child, he should be appreciated for who he is, not for what they plan for him to be. Unconditional love comes to mind at this point.

Chapter 17

THE CRUELEST WORDS OF ALL

I wish I was connected to my parents through birth and not adoption. Maybe then I wouldn't doubt myself so much.

Sally S., age 12

You are not my real mother—you are not my real father.

The words, "You are not my real mother" or "You are not my real father" can cut like a sharp knife. After putting in years of love and sacrifice, these are not the words adoptive parents like to hear.

Of course, the first reaction on the part of the parent is strong anger and resentment. Once the anger wears off, the hurt can devastate the parent. To make matters worse, often, a child will add "I hate you" to the above insult.

Even though adoptive parents know they may hear these words one day from their child, it is not easy to hear them. Parents feel unjustly belittled and attacked. Like all situations in life, people absorb words and actions from their own point of view. Adoptive parents feel betrayed when hearing their angry child denounce them.

Like so many instances in life, if we just get inside the head of the other person, we usually learn we are just the target of someone else's problem. We are not the problem; we just happen to be in the way. We are there and provide a convenient target.

The denouncement of parenthood by an adopted child almost always is said in anger and frustration, and is a reflection of low self-esteem. What the child is truly asking is, "Are you my parent?" This confrontation comes when the child is unhappy about himself and needs reassurance that his parents will stick by him and always be his parents. He never had this guarantee from his birth parents, and when he feels unworthy, he needs this reassurance from his adoptive parents.

Unfortunately, when a child verbally attacks, the adoptive parents are reeling from the insult and don't feel much like saying comforting things to their child. However, this is what needs to be done.

People who stay in a birth family know that is where they will always be—for good or bad. People who have had their birth family taken from them can actually think that no relationship is permanent. Their trust factor has been shattered. If you can't trust your own birth parents, then whom can you trust? An adopted child can verbally attack his adoptive family when he feels insecure, and the answer back will tell him a lot about his security and the trust factor within his family.

The Morgan's had three daughters; two biological daughters and a younger adopted daughter, Julie. By the time Julie was thirteen, she was causing trouble by letting her school work slip, running with the wrong crowd, and acting defiant. Her family was often reminded in their adoption support group to get inside their daughter's head to try and identify what she was feeling and trying to express during the times she acted out. This was hard for the parents because their older daughters gave them little trouble, and they felt resentment that Julie was causing so many family problems.

At one support group meeting they told of Julie coming home one day after being with a friend whom the parents did not approve of. Julie eagerly reported that her friend's mother told her that if she only had more money she would adopt Julie. This is a new twist on, "You are not my mother."

Julie's parents, upon hearing this, had all the same emotions and anger anyone would have. When the adoption support group leader asked Mrs. Morgan, "What was Julie saying to you?" Julie's mother answered, "Julie was asking me if I was really her mother or could someone else adopt her." The group agreed; Julie was asking if she was available to be adopted by someone else. She was saying, "I have been so bad, are you ready to give up on me yet?" At times like this it's natural for parents to be hurt and upset, but healthier for them to get inside their child's head and decide what he or she is *really* saying.

There is a *huge* difference between, "You are not my mother," and "Are you really my mother and will you always be, no matter what?" The words as stated are opposite from each other, but the issue involved is the same, no matter how it's stated. Fortunately, Julie's mother answered her daughter with strong expressions of family togetherness, etc. This is all Julie was asking. This is what she needed to hear.

An upset child who is down on himself may not consciously understand what he is doing, but the adults in the situation should see the underlying message. It is essential parents get their own egos and fragile feelings out of the way.

Childhood is not an easy time. Trying to figure out just who you are and what you will become can be quite intimidating. If your birth parents have already given up on you (or so the adopted child might think), what security do you have? If the adopted child attacks his adoptive parents and the parents respond to him in a loving way, a strong message is being sent. The child feels angry with himself, attacks his parents, yet gets love in return. This cycle helps to reinstate trust between the child and his world.

Chapter 18

"I'LL PROVE TO YOU I'M BAD!"

You never give away something of value, therefore I'm not of much value.
Lynn T., age 13

I must be a bad person because I was given away. I will show the world just how bad I am. I will be so bad, my adoptive parents will also give me away, and then I will have my identity. I will finally know who I am.

PARENTS NORMALLY TRY to raise their children to be good children and good citizens. Most people were raised this way and can remember the feeling of wanting to please their parents. For one thing, life was simpler at home if there was a minimum of problems. It's hard, therefore, when adoptive parents are dealing with a child who seems determined to be as bad as he can. This can be baffling.

Again, we must get inside the head of the adopted child. Fortunately, only a small percentage of adopted children fall into this behavior category. However, if parents have to deal with this syndrome for years, it is extremely taxing and difficult.

A child may test his parents for a long time. He may do something bad and find his parents deal with it, but don't throw him out. He feels he has passed that level and will then move onto the next. The child's behavior can get incrementally worse as if he is testing on one level and then another and another.

When this happens, parents must focus on loving the child and hating the behavior. The child wants to know, "How bad does my behavior need to be before my adoptive parents give me away?" As exasperating as this is, unconditional love will eventually bring the child home again. The child is always lovable although the behavior can be detestable. It seems it can take forever for some adopted children to believe this.

As a child gets into his mid-teens, he may even leave home to try to search for some identity. He is not quite sure what he is searching for, but he knows he doesn't fit where he is. He knows that he is artificially coupled with his adoptive family, and he feels he doesn't belong there. This feeling of not belonging can push him out into situations where he is hoping he will find a sense of home, a sense of belonging.

He may be old enough to realize he has to set up his own identity. He doesn't know for sure what his heritage is from his biological parents and doesn't embrace the heritage of his adoptive parents.

As mentioned in a previous chapter, the adopted child often ends up in a much lower socioeconomic situation than he had at home. He lives with people who may not have the education or advantages he has been given. Soon, he may realize he doesn't fit in the new environment either because he is accustomed to more than what he sees around him. The child may take on a part-time job, or take a class to improve himself. He will continue to advance himself to a point where he does feel comfortable, where he does feel he belongs. This may be right back on the level he was when he was living at home.

However, he discovered it himself. His present place in the world was not decided by an adoption worker or a lawyer. At this point, he has gained confidence in himself. He finally has some self-determination. Many adopted children feel powerless because when they were young and helpless, adults were making decisions for them. This difficult exercise of climbing up the socioeconomic ladder all by oneself overcomes some of this helplessness.

Brian, at the age of sixteen, left home to live in the red-light district of his city. He spent almost a year there, determined to find his biological mother whom he was convinced had been a prostitute. After awhile, Brian was tired of searching and returned home to his family. He came to the realization his birth mother may or may not have been a prostitute, but he didn't like that atmosphere and was determined to make something of himself. Brian realized that what she did with her life was not a factor in what he could do with his life. He had survived on his own in that environment and realized he had the strength to be whatever he wanted to be.

Behavior like this is extremely difficult for adoptive parents to witness. They can see their children putting themselves in harm's way over and over again. The child rejects his adoptive parents and their life-style, so will not listen to what his parents say. As is well publicized, some teens get into drugs, prostitution, and crime in order to survive. This is so contrary to their home environment that it makes parents wonder what is going on. They cannot believe their child chooses that seedy world over the loving, stable one they have provided.

In time, the child grows through that unwholesome world, if all goes well. He rises to the top of it and gets back into the main stream of society. There can be many bad experiences along the way and these can take a toll.

Mike, now in his late twenties, spent six years working his way to the top of this subculture. At the end, Mike knew he didn't want to live there. He said he learned so much there that it gave him a base of strength that he wouldn't trade for anything. To him, it was all worth it. There could be varying opinions about Mike's choices, but in his mind, this was the path he had to take even though there was a loving home waiting for him all the while.

The fact that Mike did have a loving home waiting for him undoubtedly was a source of strength for him. Adoptive parents feel there must be something they can do to rescue their child from himself. If they can do something positive, that should be the plan of action. Often, there is nothing parents can do until the child himself asks for help or finds his way back home. It's important the child knows his parents will still be there.

Having an accepting, loving home waiting surely helps the child to accelerate his journey. Even though he has made some bad decisions and used bad judgment resulting in his temporarily becoming "that bad person he always thought he was," if he is later accepted back at home, this proves to him that he is lovable after all. Hopefully, he will realize he was not given away because he was bad. After all, his adoptive parents still love and accept him. If he can see this, then he can start to work on finding the good and positive that his adoptive parents have seen all along.

One mother who went through this experience used to express it as, "It's like Todd is a tall shiny metal cylinder. All the good things we taught him are inside where we can't see them. All we can see now is the garbage he is displaying on the top. We know all that goodness is still there. He can't destroy it. He just needs to work through his garbage in order to discard it." Indeed, Todd finally did.

Chapter 19

WHAT AND WHERE AM I?

I feel like I was plucked up from one place and set down in another. I don't know who I am.
John B., age 12

How can I know where I am going if I
don't know where I came from?

One way to help a child avoid the meandering journey of "Who am I?" is to help him from a very young age in describing who he is.

Many adopted children have a hard time making decisions. They don't feel grounded enough or secure enough to make choices in life. Because their internal self-image is jumbled and wishy-washy, they look at life with that attitude. They really don't know who they are, so how can they be expected to know where they are going?

Lynn explains that her son, Sam, had a terrible time choosing from three breakfast cereals each and every morning. He had a hard time picking out clothes, needing to try on almost everything in the store before making his decision. This would take hours. Later on, Sam went through very turbulent teenage years trying to find how he fit into the scheme of life. A lack of a solidly-based identity and a muddled sense of self can make life more complicated than it needs to be.

Sometimes children like Sam need guidance and practice in making decisions. They should be coaxed into decision making so that it becomes more and more comfortable for them. They may need patient coaching at the beginning, but as they gain confidence it should become easier and easier. Constant praise is needed along the way. Sally, age fifteen, bought a pair of shoes on her own and brought them home for her parents to see. Her father commented on them, but did not give the praise Sally was expecting. She threw the shoes down the stairs as she exited to her room in tears, saying, "I can't even pick out a pair of shoes right."

Sally lacked a sense of herself. She agonized over her shoe selection and then still was questioning herself. Had she been self-confident, her father's lack of overt praise might have been no more than a minor irritation for her. However, Sally was confused as to what she wanted. She thought she knew, but questioned her decision when she saw her father's lack of enthusiasm.

Some adopted children need extensive help in sorting out who they are. A way to move through this confusion is to explore with your child all the positive avenues in which he shows an interest. Give him a sense of identity early in his life.

A biological child may see a particular interest or talent within his family. He may want to pursue this for himself to see if he, also, has this talent.

The adopted child has no such role models to emulate. He has adoptive family members, but their genes are different from his. Here is where adoptive parenting becomes different. An adopted child should be allowed to try many avenues—and also be allowed to drop out of those same avenues. He potentially will dabble in many more areas because the whole world is out there for him. He has no guidelines built in for him. It's a trial and error method.

Just because there is a talent in a biological family, that does not mean every family member has it, however the inclination may be strong to pursue similar interests. The adopted child may also want to pursue an interest that is strong within his adoptive family. This may or may not work out. If he strongly wants it to work, and he finds he has little ability for it, this becomes another separating factor, making him feel he is different from his adoptive family. He may think their biological child would have had that talent, he doesn't, and so he is a disappointment to his parents.

The adopted child is unique. He is one of a kind, as we all are. This should be emphasized over and over again for the child. He is who he is and what he makes of himself. If he has positive encouragement to follow his interests, and permission to drop them along the way of his inquiring journey, he will find his unique niche. He needs to have permission from his family to quit a quest without being labeled a quitter. He is exploring, doing research in a way. Not everything is going to work out, but he needs to keep going. He needs to feel he has his own set of gifts and talents to pursue.

This may be a frustrating time for the child if he does not find early success. Here is where parents should be alongside him encouraging him to find his own identity. We are all different from one another, but often the adopted child wants to find ways he will fit into his adoptive family and not feel like an outsider.

With sincere encouragement, parents should give the message to their child that it is all right to be different. He may feel he needs permission to do this. The child needs to feel loved and appreciated for who he is and needs to feel that love and appreciation are solidly there even though he may be different from his family. He may be on a lonelier track pursuing his innate talents and be in a field his family knows nothing about. He may feel he would be getting more sincere support were he in a family with the same talents he has. A child may feel distant from his adoptive family, again reminded he is artificially placed, and wish he had the natural inclinations and interests of his adoptive family. Common interests are always a unifying factor.

However, this can be an exciting journey, exploring many avenues along the way. The adopted child is not bound by family expectations as a biological child might be. He is freer to explore many avenues, but he needs ongoing, strong support from his family to know they want this for him. He needs to feel free of any preconceived plans. He needs honest, open support to find his uniqueness and develop it.

Chapter 20

WHAT WOULD YOUR CHILD SAY?

*Sometimes people ask me questions about myself and I
don't know how to answer. I don't feel I'm a solid person.
If I were born into a family I'd know who I was. I'd have an
identity.*

Rosemary H., age 16

*The telltale question—How would you
describe yourself? Who are you?*

IN MY WORK WITH ADOPTIVE PARENTS, I've found one question that
always startles them. The question is, "If I were to ask your child to
describe himself or herself, what would your child say?"

All too often, parents didn't know and couldn't answer the question.
They were surprised by the question. This was an indication that probably
the child didn't know who they were, either. If a child could answer that they
were a good soccer player, drummer, or good at spelling or math, then they
had an identity. If they had to search to come up with an answer, then there
probably was a problem.

This is why it is so important to help your child find out just where his talents
and interests lie. Pursue them. They are not all going to work out, but
the child needs to know where he fits in life. He needs his own identity.

Remember, the time will come when he will realize he does not inherit
any qualities from his adoptive family. At this juncture, he will realize he
stands alone in the aspect of being genetically tied to anyone he knows. As
far as his life is concerned, he has no living relative. He needs to feel he is
somebody even though he doesn't genetically belong to his adoptive family.
He needs his very own, individual, strong sense of who he is.

As a young child, he can have an identity as a fast runner, a good bed maker, skilled with crayons or playing with a ball. Parents should help him to identify himself. This is who he is. His identity will change and develop as he develops, but at each stage he should be somebody. He needs help in cementing this because an identity gives him security.

This presents a beautiful opportunity to impress upon a child that we all are what we make of ourselves. Whether or not we are tied biologically to our family, whether we have talents or barriers thrust upon us, we all are, eventually, what we make of ourselves. Adoptive parents are presented the perfect opportunity to utilize this theory. They can emphasize that their child has no inherited baggage to hold him back. He may not know by example within his family just where his gifts may be, but he has the whole world to explore. No one can say to him or her, "I'm sure you wouldn't be able to do that because no one in our family ever has."

He is free from preconceived ideas of what he should be or where he should be going. Those of us who are earthbound by our family's histories could very well envy this freedom of choice. It can be intimidating and over-whelming knowing how many options are out there. However, if a family starts early and guides their child to where they see talents forming, all the while keeping options open, the child will feel secure in his development knowing he may fail at some endeavors and succeed at others. Actually, every child, adopted or biological, should have these choices, but inherited family history often dictates otherwise.

Now—go ask your child to describe himself or herself. You may learn just where he or she is in a quest for individual identity. You may learn what you as a parent need to do to guide your child toward a healthy sense of self.

Chapter 21

BREAKING AWAY

I really want to go off on my own, but I don't know how to
do it. I've spent my life trying to be a part of my family and
now I'm expected to be independent.
        Jerry J., age 17

How can I break the parental bonds when
I have no legs of my own to stand on?

WITHOUT CONFIDENCE and security, life skills can be more difficult to attain. We have all had the experience of interacting with people at one time or another and feeling awkward about it. Perhaps we didn't feel grounded and couldn't go ahead with confidence to say or do the things we thought we should.

Some adopted teens feel this way when going through puberty. They aren't sure who they are and don't feel secure about their position within the family or within society. They know they are supposed to draw away from their immediate families at this period in their lives, but they don't feel they are on firm enough ground to stand by themselves.

Biological children may feel this same way, but adopted children have a lack of biological ties, and separation may be more of an issue for them. Biological children, obviously, always have their biological ties and, whether they like it or not, those ties always will be a part of them. Adoptive children may feel they are free-floating, not tied to anything they know.

What happens is that the insecure adopted teen doesn't do a very good job at distancing himself. He knows he should separate himself from his family, but he feels he has spent years trying to make himself an authentic part of his family. He may be afraid to "let go" of the ties to his adoptive family sensing he will feel even more alone than he has felt in the past. The end result of all this confusion is that he may leave in a tumultuous fashion. There may be no logical transition from one stage to another. He may act out in many ways that create distancing. All the while his parents are wondering where this angry, acting-out behavior is coming from. It's easier for the child to make a sudden break rather than a slow, sequential break. It is using the same principle as pulling a tooth. The pain is worse if it is done slowly. You don't want it done, but you know it has to be done, so do it quickly and get it over with.

This is hard to witness because the child is miserable. He knows he has to be independent of his parents. All his friends are doing it, but he already feels alone, and even though he may want independence, he is afraid. He isn't sure he can stand alone.

Risk taking can occur at this point. The teenager will do things he would not ordinarily do, and upon surviving, feel more confident about himself. These principles follow for any adolescent tearing himself away from his family. The adopted child, insecure as to who he is, just has a harder time of it. His journey puts him on a longer path.

Now, if he has an identity and knows who he is, adopted or biological, he has a much easier task. He may make mistakes along the way, but his fall-back position is to his own identity, not into an empty hole. He can regroup and try another path where he may find more success. The ungrounded adopted child may fall back only to feel, once again, he isn't sure of what he is doing because he doesn't know the base from which he is starting. The biological child has a biological structure to break his fall. He is part of a history, a family. The adopted child may feel he has no bottom to hit. Without an identity, there is nothing to hold onto as he falls. The aloneness envelops him once again.

Helping a child to always feel positive about something he does will go a long way in giving him confidence. There is no such thing as starting too soon. His interests will change as he grows, but remember to ask him to describe himself. He should, at all stages of his life, have a positive answer. The parent may have to encourage him and point out his talents.

Often children look upon a gift as not being important because the talent or ability comes so easily to them. Bill and Sharon looked upon their son, Danny, as a natural engineer when, at age eight, he took apart an old-fashioned clock and put it back together again. He repaired things around the house because his father had no talent in this area. One day Danny, at age six, went into the basement and returned with a hammer and nail to repair the footrest on his little brother's high chair. The family was accustomed to living with such minor broken items, but Danny saw that it needed to be repaired. When he was praised for his work, he never saw this gift as a gift. He kept saying, "Oh, anybody can do that." His parents had to tell him over and over again how wonderful it was he could accomplish such tasks. They were never sure they convinced him, but they kept trying.

Helping your child find his talents does not mean you have to enroll him in numerous classes. Our society has a tendency to overschedule our children. There are many, many little gifts as well as strong talents we all have. Watch for these. Encourage, encourage, encourage, and then praise, praise, praise.

Chapter 22

THE SEARCH

I don't want to hurt my parents. I love them and they will always be my parents, but I need to know where I came from. I need to know some of my background. That's my right.

Mary R., age 15

The almighty search! All the child wants is the missing piece of his very own puzzle.

AN ADOPTEE'S DESIRE to search is probably one of the most misunderstood issues in adoption. The results of a search can be either wonderful or disastrous. It takes great courage to go on such a quest.

In a search, all participants in the adoption triangle are intertwined and may feel threatened. The adopted child may fear hurting his adoptive parents who may think he is looking for alternate parents. The adopted parents may feel threatened when their child looks for his birth parents believing they may lose a part or all of the child they have loved for years. The birth parents dread the potential anger and wrath of their child because they did not keep him at birth. The adoptee may fear rejection, once again, by his birth parents. All or none of the above may occur.

It takes a strong desire to search for a past. Many adoptees absolutely need to know their past in order to continue on with their future. These searchers are not planning to hurt anyone, they merely need to know who they are.

It's hard for nonadopted people to imagine not knowing one's heritage, relatives, and history. Nonadopted people have grown up with this personal knowledge. It has been a part of their lives since birth.

Adoptees are given their adopted family's heritage, but that is truly not their heritage. That is like a graft on a tree. It lives with another tree, but it is not naturally a part of it. The graft has characteristics of its own that are different from the host tree.

It is no different with people. The identity of the individual is cut off when the adopted child leaves his birth setting. He arrives in his new setting with genes and personality traits from his past, but from where in his past? What person would not want to know from what tree he was cut away? If we saw a graft on a tree that looked different from the tree, wouldn't the natural question be, "What was that limb before it was grafted? Where did it come from? What kind of a branch was it? Why was it grafted?"

Beyond a natural curiosity to gain knowledge, there can be a gaping hole in some people who need to know about their birth background. *This does not reflect on the parenting skills of the adoptive parents.* Many people think it does, but it doesn't. It is just that their child has a hole in him that needs to be filled.

All the love and success and fulfillment in life cannot snuff out the question, "Who am I and where did I come from?" These are very different issues. It's like taking a hungry child and distracting him until you think the hunger goes away. It doesn't. It may be waylaid for a time, but the gnawing of the hunger is there until it is assuaged by food. For the adopted person who needs to search, the hole will be there until birth information or contact with birth parents fulfills his need.

However, not all adoptees need to know. This difference is determined not by how good or bad the adoptive parents are, but by the personality of the adoptee. Some individuals feel complete with the lives they have and the lives they develop for themselves. Other adoptees, no matter how satisfied they are in other areas, just have to know where they came from and why they were given up for adoption.

There is really no right or wrong nor good or bad. What one person is compelled to know may not be of any interest at all to another person. It is extremely personal and individual. All views on this issue need to be respected because of the intensely personal nature of the question and the individual needs of the person. Unless we have walked in their shoes, we should not judge.

The fruits of the adoptive search may change lives forever. The search may turn out to be positive or negative. Experience has shown that most adoptees feel closer to their adoptive parents after finding their birth parents. If the answers found are not positive for the searcher, it is believed that that person may need several years to assimilate his information. But, at the end of that time, he usually has accepted his personal information, can assimilate it into his present life, and then can proceed living in a healthy way. He now knows where he came from.

Mark, a successful businessman, had a wonderful marriage and family. He always said he never had a problem with his adoption, and his life bore out that statement as witnessed by his healthy marriage and family and business success. However, in later years, Mark did search only to find both his biological parents were deceased. He again, reiterated, the information really didn't affect him one way or the other, but he was glad he had searched.

Jennifer, his wife, reminded him that in their 23 years of marriage he had never slept solidly and soundly through the night—until the day he found out just who he was and where he had come from.

Chapter 23

PERFECT PARENT???

*I wish my parents were more relaxed. They seem to work so
hard at parenting. If they weren't trying so hard, we could all
be more comfortable with each other.*

Joan S., age 16

***You don't need to be perfect to be a parent. Who would want to follow in the
footsteps of a perfect person?***

IT HAS BEEN MY OBSERVATION that adoptive parents appear to work harder at parenting skills than biological parents. There are two reasons for this. First of all, there was a time they did not think they would be parents, so now that they have a family they never, never take their children for granted. The second reason is that the child they now love could have been placed with a different family. They feel adoption is a man-made system with humans determining into which family a child will be placed. Biological parents never deal with these thoughts.

There can also be a tentativeness to adoptive parenting. Using the same two reasons mentioned above, parents can question if they were meant to be parents.

Also, when instilling religious, moral or judgment values upon their children, the silent question can arise, "If this child had been placed in another family he may have been taught different religious ideas and morals, therefore, do I really have the right to impose my thinking on him?"

When the adoptive parent says to his teenager, "No, you can't stay out until midnight tonight," he may wonder if the child is thinking, "Another parent I might have been placed with wouldn't be so strict." Biological children never deal with these thoughts because they were never *placed* in a family, they were born into a family. They may not like their parent's perceived strictness, but they have no choice as to the parents they live with.

The whole adoption issue sometimes appears to be tentative and artificial. Families are created by man-made circumstances and not by a natural order. This fact is not lost on either the parents or their children. It is not discussed, but this issue is always present. In family life, there are times and circumstances where it becomes more of an issue than at other times.

Some adoptive parents, therefore, may logically think they have to be super parents, while simultaneously wondering if they ever should have been parents at all. More than one adoptive parent when the times were tough has been heard to say, "I wonder if God knew what He was doing when He denied me children." There is no basis for this statement, but one can understand the feeling when parents feel overwhelmed by current family issues.

Adoptive parenting can be much harder than biological parenting if you believe the maxim, "The apple doesn't fall very far from the tree." The genetic make-up of an adopted child is different from the potential genetic make-up of any biological child the adoptive parents might have had. Many adoptive parents are equipped to deal with someone somewhat like themselves, but they may not be raising someone like themselves.

If one were to think of all the children in a classroom or in their neighborhood, any parent would probably decide (if given a hypothetical choice) on raising the child they bore. There may be challenges, but they know what they are, and they are somewhat familiar because they or their spouse were somewhat the same way as children. The adoptive parent is raising someone else's child. They had no choice as to genetic matter, and in many cases, do not know what the genetic tendencies are.

Most parenting mirrors in some degree the way the parent himself was raised. This methodology worked for their parents and will undoubtedly work somewhat the same way now for their children. The one forgotten element in all this is that the adopted child's temperament may not fit into this system.

Temperaments and genetic tendencies may not *fit* neatly and nicely into a long family history of, "This is the way it's always been done." A natural conflict may arise that can make adoptive parents question their methods. They think, "It worked for all of my family, what am I doing wrong that it isn't working now with my child?" The system may work well, and the adopted child may be fine, but the two together may not be compatible.

The same methods do not work for all children. Biological parents know that what works with one child may have to be altered with a subsequent child. Adoptive parents need to realize this same principle. That does not make the child nor the method wrong, they are just wrong when put together. It doesn't follow that the parent is doing a bad job of parenting, it just means they need to try something else. Adoptive parents need to feel the freedom to be able to experiment and to adjust. This may be hard for them if they are parenting tentatively and do not have confidence in their judgment and parenting skills.

All parents need to know that it's all right to be less than perfect. No parent is perfect, including adoptive parents.

Wendy tells a story about what happened when she was nine years old. Her older brother, Ben, had received a wood-burning set for Christmas. The nine-year-old wanted her initials burned into a wooden letter opener she had received that same Christmas. Ben offered to do it for her, but she knew her father would do a perfect job. Wendy was shocked when she saw that her father did, indeed, burn her initials into the letter opener, but it was not the perfect job she had anticipated.

Wendy's first feeling was one of great disappointment knowing it could not be done over again. Within a few seconds of that feeling, she looked at her father and for the first time in her young life, saw her father had done the best he could, but it was far from perfect. Wendy talks about remembering that instant and feeling the strongest love for her father she had ever felt. Wendy truly did love her daddy, imperfections and all, the truest kind of love there is. The onerous pressure to be perfect had just been lifted from her, for she too, could now be just a human being trying to do her best.

Chapter 24

THE TRUST FACTOR

I obviously couldn't trust my birth mother to take care of me. If you can't trust your own mother, who can you trust? I feel I need to look out for myself first before I think about anybody else.

Larry G., age 14

You must trust before you can risk. How does a life change when trust is gone?

IT IS EVIDENT THAT A very young child needs the security of being able to trust his parents to keep him safe. His very life is in the hands of his parents who feed and care for him. Now imagine those parents "giving him away." That isn't what happens in actuality, but that is what happens in the minds of some adopted children. They think their parents "gave them away."

What does this do to the trust factor? If his own birth parents gave him away, who in the world will he ever be able to trust again? Sometimes, a child thinks his main thrust in life is to look out for himself because he can't trust anyone else to do it. Following this line of reasoning to the conclusion that some distressed adoptees come to, is the concept that you can never get close to people because they are untrustworthy and hurtful. In order not to be hurt, the person never gets involved in a close relationship. If he finds himself too close and thinks he may be rejected, he will do the rejecting first. That way he is in control. He is not hurt again, he is doing the hurting.

When the trust factor is gone, a person cannot risk becoming attached. Parents or a marriage partner loving this individual can have the purest and strongest love, but the adult adoptee who feels he cannot trust cannot love back.

He uses people. Relationships don't last, not because the adoptee is unlovable, but because he does not take the risk to love. He may take advantage of people around him, doing more taking than giving in the relationship, and after awhile, his loved ones leave him because they want his love and trust, not his abuse.

This syndrome is typical and understandable for people who have been abused (or feel they have been abused) and never want to be hurt again. Fortunately, this applies to just a small percentage of adopted adults. Even a small percentage is too many when you consider the issue is all in their heads. They were not abused, they were not "given away," but it feels that way to them. It is very hard to convince them otherwise.

A self-fulfilling prophesy can occur when they feel they are unlovable and do not return love when it is offered to them. If they start to get involved, and the relationship ends, the person says, "See, again, I'm not loved. I won't get close again and then I won't be hurt again."

Parents usually hang on to the parent-child relationship because they love their child and cannot understand why they don't see their child returning love. Biological, as well as adoptive, parents can have this same experience. Parents have a tendency to keep acting like parents and just keep loving and loving, hoping one day their love will be returned. When it comes to a marriage partner, however, this syndrome does not make for a healthy relationship. The person who loves and is used instead of being loved in return, usually doesn't stay in that relationship.

An adoptee's strong sense of identity (discussed elsewhere in this work) is the answer. An adopted person needs to know he is lovable, he is loved, and is his own individual person worthy of that love.

The act of making an adoption plan for a baby has absolutely no bearing on the worthiness of the baby. The fact that birth parents could not keep their baby safe and healthy only describes the circumstances of the birth parents at one particular time in their lives. That is all. It describes where the birth parents were on their journey through life. The baby or child are not included in that description. However, the baby or child's future is changed forever by those circumstances.

If an adopted child or adult can stand back and see that his value is independent of the fact that his birth parents could not keep and care for him, he can go on to establish his own value to himself and the world. This can be hard for many adoptees to accomplish. Those of us who are not adopted can sympathize with this when we consider how our own identity is tied in with our heritage. Our conception of our personal value is sometimes connected to the value we place on our family members.

Biological or adopted, we are the creators of our own lives and destinies if we can see our way clear to shed labels that do not apply to us. The adopted person needs a fallback position if he starts to feel he cannot trust others. A strong sense of who he is, independent of others, can be a good base for going out into the world able to trust, hence risk, again.

If he feels tied to his birth family, he needs to see the positive side of these people. His adoptive family can help him with this. If he sees himself separate from his birth family he needs his adoptive family to nurture his identity. This identity needs to be established early in life. It will change as the person grows and develops, but he should always feel he is someone, someone of value. Thus, it follows, that someone of value is worthy of love. Once a person believes in himself, he can trust and believe in others, and this enables him to take the risk of trying to establish a loving relationship.

Chapter 25

GREAT—OR NOT SO GREAT—EXPECTATIONS

I wish my parents had more faith in me. If I were their bio-
logical child I bet they would.
            Hank R., age 12

Some adopted children say their parents
don't expect much of them.

WE LET OUR CHILDREN know all the time what we think of them. Parents are more of a mirror than we realize. Some adopted children say their adoptive parents don't expect much of them because they think they will turn out to have the same qualities as their birth parents. Children, pondering the reason they may have been given up for adoption, sometimes think of their birth parents in negative terms. At times, adopted children want to feel a bond with their birth parents. Don't give them a negative path of behavior to follow. Judging the birth parents can create a wedge in the adoption triangle.

It has been mentioned before how important it is to speak of the biological parents in positive terms. Adopted children have a natural loyalty to them. Often, when a child is down on himself and feels lonely, he has the desire to connect to his past. If he thinks of his birth parents as sexually promiscuous or drug or alcohol abusers, he may engage in that same behavior in order to feel a bond. He may feel he doesn't connect with his adoptive family, but with this deviant behavior he feels that he has something in common with his birth parents. It may well be that his birth parents were not promiscuous nor drug or alcohol abusers, but if the child thinks of them only in negative terms, it is natural he will think of them in this light.

When parents don't have high standards for their child, and the child senses not much is expected of him, he can easily arrive at the conclusion that it is because of his biological background. One reaction may be that he wants to prove his adoptive parents wrong, in which case he will work hard to excel. However, other children respond by believing they have license to do everything bad they want. Their anger and acting out will prove their adoptive parents are right. This is their self-fulfilling prophesy. The parents got the negative behavior they expected.

In the world in general, people are often misunderstood. We say one thing and the other person interprets it differently than how we had intended. Some adopted children are masters at this. It sometimes appears they twist almost all that is said and act somewhat paranoid at times.

It is so important to see the world through the eyes of the young adopted child. He may think someone has already given up on him, so sometimes may hear the least little criticism as a strong denouncement.

In talking with some insecure adopted children, parents would be surprised at the negative interpretations their children conceive. For instance, if a child hears, "Your mother was a drug addict and I don't want that for you," he may interpret this as, "My parents expect me to be a drug addict." If parents question their child about where some mislaid money might be, he may interpret the question as "They don't trust me." Some of this can happen in biological families as well, but in adoptive families children may read more into the message than their parents ever intended. Reassurance and definite clarity of message can help these situations.

A child's behavior may be bad, but parents must instill in their child that he is not bad. Detach the behavior from the child—the behavior is bad and the child is good.

Here is where high expectations come in. If parents have low expectations, it is only natural to think it's because the child is limited. Parents should express disappointment in negative behavior, while at the same time tell their child they expect better of him. His bad behavior does not match the high quality person he is. This sends the proper message.

Chapter 26

SOLID ADVICE FROM AN ADOPTEE
TO PARENTS

AS MENTIONED IN CHAPTER 1, I spent several days going over my adoption research information with one of our sons who had experienced many of the problems shared by adolescent adoptees.

At the end of our discussion I asked him what his personal thoughts were on adoption. Specifically, I asked what advice he would give to adoptive parents who are currently struggling with a child like he had been. This discussion was held one week before his 32nd birthday, so these are the thoughts of a man who had survived the troubled adopted adolescent's quagmire.

His advice and thoughts are as follows:

· Be constantly assuring without being smothering.

· When bad behavior is being displayed, don't just deal with the surface behavior. Find out what the child is trying to tell you. Get inside his head and deal with the child's reality. What is right and true or what is real, may have nothing to do with the battle at hand. What needs to be dealt with is the child's reality. It is his real world and his demons are real to him.

· The adopted child, like the biological child, needs to know both parents wanted him. If one is dominant because the other is absent much of the time due to business demands, the child's logic concludes that only one really wanted to adopt him.

· An adopted child may have an exaggerated need for what he perceives to be the complete truth. When he thinks he is not being told the whole truth, he can get a "paranoid" feeling that it's because he isn't a "real" member of the family, so is not privy to inner family information.

· The adopted child needs the reassuring balance of fact regarding his adoption, grounded by facts of his day-to-day life in his adoptive family. Both are factors in his existence. Both are real to him and need to be held in a healthy, honest balance.

· Adoptive parents need to relax. There are always going to be problems, no matter how perfect the parents try to be. If parents could look at themselves as nurturers and caretakers, there wouldn't be such a strong need for them to control.

· Be sensitive to the fact the child may, at times, feel like an outsider. Be inclusive, not exclusive. The child may read the signals all wrong and feel excluded many times when it is not justified. This doesn't matter if it seems real to the child.

· Question your motives as a parent. What were your expectations for your child? Were they realistic? What are your expectations now? Are they realistic?

· It's O.K. to let your child know you aren't perfect. He, then, likewise, has permission to be humanly imperfect.

· Be open, aware, sensitive, flexible, loving.

· Finally, parents need to realize they are not responsible for their child's happiness. The child is responsible for his own. Be a role model for your child. Take responsibility for your own actions, your own life, your own sense of fulfillment.

· The basic needs of an adopted child, like all of humanity, are acceptance, respect, and above all else, unconditional love.

Chapter 27

CONCLUSION

As mentioned in the beginning, we all have the ability within us to take our talents and strengths and nurture them, enabling us to become the person we truly want to be. This sounds simple, but we all know we are encumbered by societal and family expectations, as well as our own psychological baggage we gather throughout our lives.

We ourselves often create our own limitations. We fight our demons, real or imagined, in our journey through life. It can be so clear to another person that we are making our battle harder than it needs to be. That's easy for the other person to say because they aren't walking in our shoes, however, there can be some validity in their viewpoint.

I think every work about adoption should make note of those parents who have been wonderful, loving parents, and still their child (even as an adult) causes problems for himself and others. As adoptive parents we take on unknown genetic material that at times can cause serious behavioral problems. Some parents have spent an inordinate amount of effort, energy, and money in helping their child. In spite of this, in a small percentage of cases, the child goes from childhood to adulthood with his issues unresolved.

The parents I've seen in counseling almost always come with the attitude, "We've done something terribly wrong and we don't know how to fix it." In the best of circumstances, they leave counseling with the attitude, "We did not do anything wrong, but we now know how to fix the problem." There are times, however, when facts dictate that the parents did nothing wrong, and they are not the ones to fix it. This latter position, of course, is the hardest for them to live with.

Their child's attitude is the problem. Adoptive parents can do everything right, and still their child will fight the concept of adoption, never coming to grips with the fact he was given away. These are sad cases because everyone loses. The child may have wonderful, loving, caring parents and never see this reality. There is one definition of hell that seems appropriate here. "Hell is being in heaven and not knowing it." This can happen in the case of some adopted children, and only they can change their way of thinking. They are already in a wonderful place and only need to open their eyes.

Parents need to remember they have already made an extraordinary effort in raising their child. If there are still problems by the time their child is an adult, parents need to let go. They can be there physically, spiritually, and lovingly for their child, but they need to let go of the responsibility for his behavior. In all probability, their child would have the same problems no matter what adoptive family had loved him.

Adopted or not, we all have a lifetime of issues to work through. The principles discussed in this book are universal. Understand the other person, try to get inside his head, imagine how he is feeling, empathize, support, and help him along his journey.

None of us has the ability to perceive the other person's challenges. Too often in life, people take the stance of discounting another person's issues, often dismissing them as trivial or imagined. This is a pretentious attitude when you consider none of us knows the road the other person has already traveled. In actuality, most people are doing the best they can with the circumstances life has dealt them. People try to keep their painful issues hidden, out of sight so they think, but issues manifest themselves in behavior and aren't hidden at all. Often, we judge their behavior without understanding their issues. It would be better if we saw their behavior as a window into their inner self. We all need validation and support no matter where we are in our journey.

A friend of mine paid me a compliment one day, and after my thanking her, she said, "Well, my mother used to say it's better to give flowers to the living than give flowers to the dead." That's a simple concept, a beautiful concept.

Even though we can't fully comprehend the issues our adopted children live with because we have never traveled their road, the least we can do is respect the path they are on, travel it beside them as best we can, and give them flowers along their way. Hopefully, early in their journey, their storm will subside just like the March ice storm, and they will experience the peace that follows.

Finally—I began the book with this thought, and I would like to conclude with the same thought. It is the responsibility of every parent, as well as teachers and counselors, to help each child realize that he is unique. Help him cut all negative ties to his past—someone gave me away, someone hurt me, or someone didn't love me. These facts in no way determine his value. He, alone, determines that.

Part 3

COUNSELING HANDOUTS

Following are some of the handouts used in counseling support sessions with adoptive parents who were seeking help in interacting with their children. Each handout makes a point on a specific subject.

Most of the handouts that follow contain information that has already been discussed within the book. This just puts the material in a more succinct format and may be of additional help to adults dealing with adopted children.

BASICS OF DISCUSSION

In order to understand our adopted children we need to get inside their minds. What are they thinking? Why are they thinking this way? For the vast majority of adoptive parents, this is a new area because they themselves were biological children, not adopted children.

In gaining insight into an adopted child's thinking, this does not comment one way or the other on issues of right and wrong, good and bad. An example of this would be if a man went into a store and stole milk and bread to feed his children. If you explained to the store owner afterwards that the man had lost his job and was destitute, and the reason he stole was to feed his family—you are not justifying the theft. The storekeeper is understandably angry and could well accuse you of trying to defend the thief. In fact, you have given no judgment at all. You reported on the factual reason why the man stole, the cause of the action. You have identified the motivation for the action. You have not justified the action. It is easy for the offended person who is angry to attach a value judgment to your explanation. His emotions (anger and resentment) are leading him to this.

So it can be with parents in discussions regarding their troubled children. In explaining probable causes for their child's behavior, the parent can take the defensive stand that you are defending the child, are on the child's side so to speak. This must be remembered in an adoption support group. *There are no sides.* There is only a common goal of trying to restore harmony to a home. There is confusion and pain on both the child's and the parent's side.

The goal here is to reduce the pain, and this can only be done by the parent removing himself from his own personal pain and anger and resentment so that he can concentrate on understanding the thinking of his troubled adopted child. As long as the parent holds onto his own anger, he cannot move ahead to a harmonious, loving solution. It's essential that the parent change his own attitude before he can help his child change. The parent in all likelihood is not responsible for his child's problems, but he can be responsible for his child's change. Holding onto your own anger as a parent impedes working through any issues. While you are angry you are defensive. You have the choice to hold onto your negative emotions, but if you can get out of yourself and see the whole of the situation, this new perspective will put you in control of changing behavior. While you are emotional you cannot do this. The choice is yours.

This in no way implies that your anger is not justified. It undoubtedly is, however, as long as you embrace it you cannot move ahead, and you surely cannot help your troubled child. Some hold onto their anger with righteous indignation feeling they have been betrayed by their child, the adoption agency, and life itself. This is their choice, but unless they get tired of feeling this way and want to feel better, they can have many years of stagnation.

Another way to look at this would be to imagine yourself as a teacher. There is one boy in your class who is disruptive. Let's say he feels different from the others, feels he doesn't fit in, just doesn't feel comfortable with himself. Let's say he is unusually short. Now, you as the teacher can treat him just like everyone else—and you will be getting the same disruptive behavior. As the saying goes, if you keep doing what you are doing, you will keep getting what you are getting. You have another choice. You can give the child special tasks to do to increase his sense of identity, praise him, encourage his special talents, or do whatever is appropriate to make him feel he does fit in, he is a good person.

There are choices here. We as parents face the same situation. We say we are treating our children equally, but, we know when a child falls down and skins his knee, at that moment we are tending to a hurting child. If we can get some insight into the mental and psychological "skinned knees" within our child's mind, we can attend to them, also. Because we can't see physical evidence of these "bruises" or because our child doesn't come to us and describe his pain, it's hard for us. Our children show us their pain by their behavior, often negative. It is our job to decode that behavior. What is the child feeling when he misbehaves? Why is he doing it? What is the source of his anger?

We have never experienced these particular "mental bruises" because we have never been adopted. What we see is disruptive, negative behavior and for the most part, we have no idea where it is coming from. So, when we look into the causes of this behavior, let's remember we are not defending or justifying the behavior, we are merely explaining cause and effect like the example of the man stealing food for his children. No right or wrong, no good or bad, just cause and effect.

Once we, as parents, understand the cause of our children's behavior, we can then intercede intellectually instead of emotionally. We no longer need to carry our anger or resentment or frustration around with us. We can shed these negative emotions and approach our situation from an intellectual cause and effect basis. This is not always easy because we are human, too. However, we need to change our attitudes and reactions to our children in order to help them change their behavior. We are the adults here. This is our challenge.

FACTUAL DIFFERENCES BETWEEN BIOLOGICAL AND ADOPTED CHILDREN

Biological	Adopted
two parents	*four parents*

Adopted child has two mothers to accept or reject, emulate, or discard. Has two fathers to accept or reject, emulate, or discard. All of these are considered in the journey to find adoptee's identity. There are many more choices for the adopted child. "More confusion as to Who am I? Whose child am I?"

Biological	Adopted
related siblings	*unrelated siblings*

An inherent sense of belonging, of closeness is caused by knowledge that siblings have some similar genetic material. Adopted children have no more physical connection to their brothers or sisters than they do to their friends or schoolmates. Think of the person sitting next to you, then think of your brother or sister. Do you feel a difference in closeness? The adopted child has no blood relative.

Biological	Adopted
Physical characteristics similar within family.	*No "hand me down" physical traits.*

Studies show parents tend to feel closer to a child who physically resembles them. There is binding/bonding factor to having Uncle Dick's nose, Aunt Mary's eyes, etc. This conversation is totally absent from the life of an adopted child. There is never any mention of who he/she takes after. The child stands genetically alone, all by himself.

Biological	Adopted
Personality/interest/talent traits are binding/bonding issues.	*Personality/interest/talent traits are reminder that child is "apple from another tree." Can be separating factor.*

This intensifies over the years as differences become more developed/distinct.

A larger variance is possible in physical traits, temperament, athletic, or artistic ability. There is always the possibility an athletic parent wants an athletic, physically coordinated child, not a musician or artist.

Biological	Adopted
Born into circumstances— like it or not. Natural order.	*Artificially placed into circumstances.*

"Born into" equals inherent right to be where you are and who you are. You have a place to start in building and developing yourself into what you want to become. The adopted child's placement decision, made by adults, could be right or wrong, good or bad, appropriate or inappropriate. The decision can *always* be questioned, was there a better choice?

Biological	Adopted
Task in teen years to decide what part of his heritage he wants to keep, embrace.	*Doesn't belong in his heritage. Could be in another family. How to choose from unfounded base.*

Adolescent years are when the adopted child becomes cognitive of his artificiality within his family structure. Placement decision was made by man, not by God or nature. This was not the natural order of life. This realization can shake a child, question his bonds to his family, make him feel very alone and angry. It takes away his base. He wants to launch himself, dive into life, but now his diving board is shaky. He does not stand on firm ground, facts of his existence are not secure, they are questionable.

Biological	Adopted
Was never given away by mother to strangers.	*Was given away by mother to strangers.*

It happened once, it can happen again. Very logical. Adoptive parents can give him away. Boyfriend, girlfriend, spouse can give him away, reject him. Can have lifelong difficulty trusting people. If own birth mother gave him away, he thinks he can therefore be rejected by every other human being he deals with. His own mother proved to him he was not worth keeping.

ESSENTIAL KEYS TO PROBLEM SOLVING

1. GET INSIDE YOUR CHILD'S HEAD. WHERE IS HE/SHE COMING FROM?

2. WHAT IS HIS/HER BEHAVIOR TELLING YOU? WHAT IS HE REALLY TRYING TO SAY?

3. GET OUT OF YOURSELF! DON'T BE DEFENSIVE, PARANOID. DON'T TAKE THINGS PERSONALLY. YOUR CHILD'S ANGER HAS TO BE DIRECTED AT SOMEONE– AND YOU ARE A GOOD TARGET. CONSIDER YOUR CHILD'S FEELINGS BEFORE YOUR OWN. YOU ARE THE ADULT.

4. YOUR CHILD DOESN'T KNOW YOU WILL ALWAYS BE HIS/HER PARENT. TESTS CAN GO ON AND ON UNLESS HE KNOWS.

5. YOUR FEELINGS (NEGATIVE) ARE NORMAL. YOUR CHILD'S FEELINGS (NEGATIVE) ARE NORMAL.

6. YOUR MARRIAGE IS PARAMOUNT! DON'T LET CHILD SPLIT YOU. WORK TOGETHER. "THESE THINGS, TOO, SHALL PASS."

HANDLING YOUR ANGRY CHILD

When your child expresses anger toward you or argues with you, you may feel that he is angry with you. That's natural.

Usually, our first reaction is to take it personally. We may feel many emotions at this time, and in all probability, none of them positive. Often, our anger rises to a pitch to match the child's. We, of course, feel we are right, and also, as the parent we have the upper hand. Reacting with matched anger usually is not productive. Your child still feels his anger even though you have told him it's wrong and unjustified. This scenario can be acted out over and over again in a household.

There is another way to handle this issue. You, indeed, have choices which are listed below. If your child is verbally attacking you, you have three choices:

1) You can feel insulted, hurt, angry or resentful and respond accordingly.

2) You can think your child is foolish and overreacting, and just ignore him.

3) You can wonder where his anger (displaced in your mind) is coming from. It appears to be real to him. You honestly feel you don't deserve the wrath of his anger. It's intensity might be very strong. In order to help your child get emotionally balanced again (so you won't be the target again—or at least not as intensely) you can help him analyze the source of his anger. There is always a source, perceived or real, for our emotions. If you think you are not the cause, isn't it logical for you to help your child understand the true cause—the real, deep source? This should be done unconditionally and with nonjudgment, calmly and lovingly.

If his anger is explosive and intense, plan a time later to discuss it. He may not be able to talk rationally at the moment his anger has a hold on him. Do not say his anger is unjustified. His anger may well be, indeed, very justified. It's just that it is misplaced with you. Help him understand its source so that it can be dissipated or expressed in a healthier way.

PARENTING TOOLS

Give your child one *honest, direct, sincere* compliment each day. Include a hug with it. Direct means no backhanded remarks like, "That's not bad" or "I didn't think you could do something that good" or "You surprised me by how well you did." These are *NOT* compliments. Instead say, "That's wonderful!" or "I knew you could do something that good" or "That's no surprise to me. I knew you'd do a great job."

Emphasize **verbally** the cohesiveness of your family. You assume you will always be a family. Adopted children do not necessarily assume this.

Express verbally and physically not only unconditional love, but unconditional *appreciation*. Being appreciated is as important as being loved.

Be approachable. You don't need to be perfect. If you express your imperfection along with the fact you are always trying to do better, you have just given your child the right to be imperfect—along with the expectation he/she will, also, always try to improve. The process of trying and improving is the key—being perfect is not the key.

In all situations where your child is misbehaving, ask yourself, "What is my child trying to tell me through this behavior?" It may appear to be anger, disdain, sadness, or indifference. What is your child trying to express through this negative behavior. Look beyond what appears on the surface. Often your child doesn't know the motivation for his negative feelings. He just feels bad. He may feel excluded, angry at his situation, sad at his loss (of birth parents), vulnerable (does he really belong anywhere?), inferior (his birth parents must be terrible people), or insecure (is he the child of his adoptive parents or his birth parents?). An adopted child often wonders who he is. During adolescence this can be stressful because it's at a time when most teens are developing their sense of self.

Help your child feel free from guilt. They innately feel that they are "messing up" because of their inner feelings—insecure, tentative within the family setting, angry at a system which separated them from biological parents. Help them realize that whatever they feel is **normal.** No guilt is necessary. As parents you can support them through their journey, their journey for identity. They are who **they** are. They can develop themselves. They have concrete adoptive parents and phantom biological parents to mirror, but in the end, they are who they make themselves to be. We are all responsible for ourselves.

PARENTING GOALS

COMPETENCE–IMPORTANCE–RESPONSIBILITY

Help your child:

Gain a feeling of competence—(even though he/she is not as good as you would like). Praise them for their ability for what they already can do.

Gain a feeling of their own importance—within your family dynamics. Give them a feeling of security within your family circle.

Gain a feeling of responsibility. There are consequences for their behavior—and they are in charge. They are responsible for what they do.

KEY POINTS IN ADOPTIVE PARENTING

1. YOU WILL ALWAYS BE HIS PARENT. Reassure your child in subtle ways (and strong ways when needed) that you will always be his parent. You know you will, but he doesn't know that. After all, a parent has already abandoned him, why not again, why not you? Do not assume because all is going lovingly and smoothly in your family that he does not think of this.

2. INNER SENSE OF LOSS. Because of his being abandoned originally, the adopted child often has an inner sense of loss. This is hard for non-adopted people to empathize with. It's hard for the adopted child or adult to verbalize. They just say it feels like they have a hole inside them. In trying to fill up this hole, the adopted child may feel he never gets enough attention as a child, and as a teenager may take on drugs or alcohol to dull his pain. Food, also, may be a substitute for feeling a lack of love. It doesn't need to be real, but their perception is real.

Adoptive parents often say they are constantly reassuring their adopted child, but the need goes on and on. The child appears to need constant, never ending reassurance. Sometimes the hole is so deep it seems it will never be filled up, but parents need to be tireless and vigilant in the support they give their child.

3. ARE YOU MY MOTHER/FATHER? When an adopted child in anger or fear says, "You are not my mother/father!" he is, in fact, asking "ARE you my mother/father?" This statement is made when a child feels vulnerable and alone and needs strong reassurance right then that no matter what happens in the family, you as a parent are, indeed, his mother/father.

It's natural for adoptive parents to be personally hurt when their child attacks them in this manner. Instead of feeling betrayed, get inside your child's head and try to feel his emotions. He is, undoubtedly, angry or frustrated at something and feels at this point that he is not even a legitimate part of your family—a terrifying sensation for a child. Believe it or not, it's at this point that he needs a loving hug.

4.TENTATIVE PARENTING. Adoptive parents often have a tendency to parent tentatively. They think their decisions are arbitrary because their being their child's parent was, also, an arbitrary decision. All children need constant, firm, loving guidelines and boundaries. You may not always be right, but no one is.

5. SENSE OF WHO HE IS. The adopted child (much more so than the biological child) needs a sense of who he is. The biological child knows early on who he belongs to because of his birth. He has an unbreakable link to his identity. The adopted child's link has already been broken. He spends time and energy searching emotionally and intellectually for some grounding. Adoptive parents can help immeasurably with this process by being truthful about what they know of their child's biological past (*always positive*), and then help him explore any interests and pursue any talents he may express. After all, he doesn't know if he comes from a line of musicians or a line of carpenters. The adopted child needs (1) encouragement to try all sorts of things and (2) the strong message that we all are what we make of ourselves. Our lineage may be important, but the bottom line is what we do with our own lives. If your family is athletic, your child needs your expressed encouragement it's O.K to be a book worm. If your family is musical your child does not need to be. He needs to find his own comfort zone with your unconditional and enthusiastic support.

6. TESTING THE LIMITS. The adopted child may do more testing of limits than the biological child. He may think he is bad or came from a bad background. Will you still keep him as your child if he displays bad behavior?

Unfortunately, one test is not enough. Once you have accepted him with a little "badness," he will escalate his behavior just to see how far he can go before you, too, give him away. All a parent can do is say that you will not tolerate bad behavior, but you will always love him in spite of his bad behavior, and you will always be his parent. This stage can hit in the preteen and teenage years when there are already many other issues to be handled.

This stage can go on for years because your child may view himself as a bad person. Does anybody ever give away something of value? He was given away. Does that make him valueless?

7. ACCEPT YOUR CHILD'S FEELINGS AND THOUGHTS AS REAL. They are real to him. Discounting them or belittling them will only cut off communication because your child will think you don't understand. An adoptive parent needs to validate their child's sense of loss, anger at being abandoned, and sense of not being in control of their own destiny. At the same time, parents need to provide a steady, secure, loving presence for their child.

8. ACCEPT THE FACT THAT YOUR CHILD HAS TWO OTHER PARENTS. This is a hard one. Adoptive parents do not feel their child is any less their child because he is adopted and not biological. There are biological and genetic differences, however. As the child matures, these differences become more pronounced. The differences must be accepted and nurtured (assuming they are positive).

9. SEARCHING. When your child asks about his background or, when older, actually searches for his biological family, this has *nothing* to do with you as adoptive parents. He is merely trying to find out his identity to fill in some of the loss he feels. He is a mystery to himself and needs some answers to help him mature. As one adopted adult said, "How can I know where I am going if I don't know where I came from?"

10. BE INCLUSIVE, NOT EXCLUSIVE. The adopted child may be sensitive to the fact that he does not biologically belong to your family. Be aware of situations where he may feel like an outsider i.e., discussions of inherited traits of other family members, talk of your family heritage, keeping information from him, etc.

Just because adoption is not an issue with you as a parent, do not assume it is not an issue with your child.

11. ADOPTION THOUGHTS. A group of happy, well-adjusted adolescents were asked how often thoughts of their adoption came up in their daily lives. The answers ranged from "once every day" to "all the time." This was a surprise to people in the adoption field. It is obviously more of an issue with adopted children than with adoptive parents. Parents need to be aware of this. Being adopted is a state of being, it does not go away. It is not good nor bad, it just is a permanent state of being.

12. NURTURE, NURTURE, NURTURE! Remember you are the adult. You may feel frustrated or angry or unappreciated at times, but it's your child's journey that is important. His journey may be a difficult one, but your being aware of its pitfalls can be essential to helping him along his way. Your steadiness and unfaltering, unconditional love can make a difference in how he lives out his adult years.

DO'S, DON'TS, WHY'S AND WHY NOT'S

Following are some ideas regarding issues that arise in adoptive families. There are some commonly held concepts that people have accepted, but experience has shown these concepts may not be accurate. These and other issues are explained below:

1. Don't
Don't say "Your mother loved you enough to give you up."

Why not?
Some young children have asked their adoptive parents, "When will you love me enough to give me up?" A child is too young to understand the "giving up" aspect of adoption. In their young minds they may equate loving with giving away. Often, this is one of the first phrases adoptive parents say to their child about adoption. Adults understand this concept, but it is a little deep for children, and they take the words at face value.

---

2. Do
Be very careful in using "time outs" with an adopted child.

Why?
In using "time out" as punishment for a small child, the message is "You will be isolated from the family because of your bad behavior." There is nothing in and of itself that is wrong with this technique, however with an adopted child, there can be an insidious message. The child hears "I will be sent away from my family if my behavior is bad." Again, we are working with a young child who cannot truly understand the whole concept. Parents mean to do this for a particular incident, but the child sometimes hears this for his whole being.

One of two behaviors can result. A testing pattern can be set up by the child to see just how much his parents love him. How bad does his behavior need to be before he is sent away permanently? The timid, insecure child may act like a perfect child, doing everything his parents want of him because of his fear of being sent away. He may bury many behaviors which are natural progressions in the growing up process. This is not healthy.

3. Don't
Don't try to mold your child into your image.

Why not?
Everyone has values and standards which are dictated by family and society. These are essential. However, when it comes to the individuality of a person, there are many innate gifts buried in each of us. These should be allowed to surface and be nurtured whether they fit comfortably into the current family structure or not. Each child deserves to be able to develop himself. He should not be molded into a someone he is not, in order to adjust to the rest of the family.

4. Do
Tell your child over and over he is a permanent part of your family.

Why?
He was "given away" once, and in his mind anything that has happened once, can happen again. This is a frightening concept for adults to realize. Many an adoptive parent has been told by an adopted child (now adult), that when they were young they didn't feel like they would always be in the family. Why? Because nobody ever told them. This is a shock to adoptive parents. They didn't tell their child because it was not an issue. Of course, they will always be a part of their family. The adoptive parents went through so much to have a child, the thought that the relationship would end never enters their head. But, it does enter your child's head. **Tell him!!** You are all bonded together **forever.**

P.S. No matter how bad his behavior is.

5. Do
Do speak positively about your child's birth parents.

Why?
Your child derives part of his self value from what he knows about his birth parents. He may think that if they are not good people, then there is little chance of his being a good person. At times, adoptive parents need to

selectively edit some background information they know about the birth parents, but the positives can always be emphasized.

---

6. Do

Accept the fact that your adopted child has four parents.

Why?

Your child *does* have four parents. This is a fact. Your child knows it, and family life can run more smoothly if adoptive parents accept it. Birth parents are phantom parents and not in the forefront of life, however they do exist. Adoptive parents are working with the product of the gene pool of the birth parents. In some cases this presents many challenges to adoptive parents (where there is a wide variation in temperament, talents, etc. from the adoptive family).

---

7. Do

Praise, praise, praise.

Why?

Your child needs to know he is accepted, loved, cherished and appreciated to his very core for the person he is. An adopted child often needs more verification of who he is. His uniqueness may be quite different from other members of his family, and this fact may make him feel like an outsider. He needs to be praised for the person he innately is. Biological children by definition belong to the family, an adopted child needs to hear he belongs even though he may be somewhat different from other members.

---

8. Do

Create an atmosphere within your family whereby your child can comfortably talk with you about his adoption.

Why?

As your child grows up he will need different levels of information about himself. He may be comfortable at a certain age, and then, a few years later, as he develops, he may need further clarification about his background. Family dynamics should always be such that he is comfortable asking for answers. If adoptive parents appear comfortable talking about adoption, this can set the comfort level for their children. Usually, adoptive parents don't know all the answers their child needs, but they can create a sense of support and encouragement for their child.

9. Do

Be very, very sensitive to your child's sense of loss.

Why?

This is another of the issues where most adoptive parents are in the dark. The adopted child has already lost his birth parents. This is on a deep, subconscious level, but it exists. When the family moves, a friend moves away, the child changes schools, a pet dies, or a family member moves away or dies; all these are times when many adoptive parents are surprised at the reaction of their child. They are not aware that a healed-over wound has been reopened. Once again, someone or something has been taken from them. They can be overly sensitive, feel the loss deeply, and are in need of strong support from those who love them.

---

10. Don't

Exclude your child verbally.

Why not?

Adopted children can be sensitive to phrases like, "He looks just like his father. She plays the piano like her mother. Of course, he'll be as tall as his father. He's an athlete just like his father." These comments are so common in our everyday life. We can't stop saying them, but we can be sensitive to the adopted child within hearing distance who won't be compared to his parents because we have no birth parent information. This can make a child feel different from others, not a true part of the family.

We need to be aware and alert. Often, this is a time to make a statement about everyone's uniqueness. This can help to level the playing field.

---

11. Don't

Fall into the trap of over-control when it comes to your child.

Why not?

It is extremely common for adoptive parents to feel the need to closely control their adopted child. This comes from several sources. The background of their child may not be known, and the sense is that they may need to "mold" this child a little more than they would their biological child. Also, the emotional toll that goes into adoption can be close to overwhelming, and parents don't want anything to go wrong now that they finally have their child.

Adoptive parents are just as perfect and imperfect as biological parents. Parenting is an art and not a science. A relaxed, confident approach is often the best. Adoptive parents don't need to prove anything to anybody.

12. Don't

Don't compare an adoptive family to a biological family.

Why not?

A family who has adopted children has different issues than a family who has biological children. The vast majority of issues are the same, but adopted children and adoptive parents face issues that a biological family will never face. This must be accepted by adoptive parents. There can be more challenges.

13. Do

From early on, give your child a strong sense of identity.

Why?

Because an adopted child was not born into his family, he may need his own sense of identity to be stronger than the biological child who derives part of his identity from his family. As the adopted child grows up, he realizes he has no blood ties to his adoptive family. Since his birth information may be slight, he needs to feel he is a strong person of and by himself. Adoptive parents have the ongoing opportunity to encourage this feeling. Again, the uniqueness factor of all human beings is an issue here.

14. Don't

Don't punish behavior without analyzing its cause.

Why not?

This is no different than with all children, adopted or not. However, in the case of an adopted child, bad behavior may come from a testing pattern whereby the child is purposely doing bad things to see how strong his parents love is and at what point, they will give him away (like his birth parents did). Deal with the cause, not just the surface behavior.

15. Do

Understand that your adopted child is aware of his adopted status even when he doesn't talk about it.

Why?

The adopted status of their child is of little or no consequence to adoptive parents. They, therefore, think the adopted status is of little or no consequence to their child. This idea is "verified" by a parent saying, "My child never talks about being adopted, so it doesn't make any difference to him." It does. Studies have shown that the adoption factor is indeed, a factor, in the life of the adoptee. This is not good nor bad, it is just one factor in their life. In extreme cases, it can be debilitating causing unhealthy behavior, but this is rare. However, don't discount the fact that an adoptee is constantly reminded by society that he is unusual.

16. Do

If your child shows angry behavior, understand its source.

Why?

Sometimes, adopted children exhibit angry behavior that seems to come from nowhere. Remember, they may feel that when they were babies, they were pawns in a system set up by society whereby a person who could not provide for their baby could secure a loving family for that baby. The baby was never consulted. He was helpless.

This can be a source of general anger in the teenage years of an adoptee. They can feel resentful at a system that placed them *arbitrarily* in a family not their own. There is no way they can get back at the original people who caused this, so adoptees appear to be angry at the world that would do this to them. They were helpless at the time, but they can express their feelings now.

17. Don't

If your child steals, don't dismiss it as surface behavior.

Why not?

Antisocial behavior always has a cause. Some adopted children who have been caught stealing have said, "Someone stole my parents away from me when I was a baby, so now it's my turn to steal from someone else. It's O.K. because it was done to me."

18. Do

Accept your child for his uniqueness.

Why?

Your child has a right to be himself—whether he fits neatly into the adoptive family or not. His 'different' behavior may not be rebelliousness, it may just be his differences developing. Your child needs acceptance for his differences. He needs verbally reassuring permission to be himself. Allow him and encourage him to explore as many avenues as he may be interested in. Remember, he has no family history or guidelines as to where his talents may lie. His range is not defined by the adoptive family's range.

---

19. Do

Assure and reassure your adopted child if he needs it.

Why?

It is commonly heard in adoption support groups that parents are very tired of reassuring their adopted child over and over again. They comment that they encourage and reassure, and then the next day are asked to do it again. By the teenage years, parents are worn out. It does seem that some adopted children seem to need this extra effort by parents. It appears to be a genuine need for reinforcement.

---

20. Do

Understand the translation of "You are not my parent !"

Why?

This statement which too many adoptive parents hear is not at all what it appears to be on the surface. Obviously, it is said in anger. What parents don't realize is that the anger is usually turned inward onto an insecure child beseeching his parent for a loving answer to, "Are you really my parent and will you always be my parent?" At a time like this, often the parent is also angry and not in the mood for a loving answer.

However, if a parent (the adult here) can get his own injured ego out of the way and hear his child's plea for reinforcement, he'll be able to give the right answer. "Yes, I am your parent, and no matter what you do, I will always love you and I will always be your parent." This is what the child is begging to hear. He just doesn't know how to ask.

21. Do

When the appropriate time comes, help your child leave home.

Why?

Some adopted children have spent years trying to fit into their adoptive family, and now society says it is time to leave. This seems to be contrary to where their efforts have been spent. When the connection doesn't seem easy or natural, adopted children can expend great energy trying to find ways to belong to their families. They realize these ways are more or less man made, not biological. The ties, therefore, may seem less binding. When adoptees leave home, there may be a question in their minds as to whether these ties are strong enough to last.

This may be another time in the life of your child where reassurances are needed. Distance does not break up a loving family. A family is always there for each other, even across miles of separation.

22. Do

Support your child in his search for his birth parents.

Why?

This can be extremely hard for adoptive parents to do. They have a natural fear of losing their child to a new found birth parent. Adoptive parents can think, "Aren't we enough for you? Why do you need another parent?"

Adoptive parents need to understand the search for one's roots has nothing to do with the adoptive family. This search is done in the most perfect and loving of adoptive families as well as in unsuccessful adoptive families. This is merely a human being wanting to know who he is. A part of his human puzzle was denied him at birth, and he now wants this piece of himself. It will complete him, not drive him from the only family he has.

Even if he connects with a part of his birth family and has a relationship with them, experience has shown the adoptee usually has a stronger relationship and commitment to his adoptive family than he had before the search. Adoptive parents know where they came from. Is it fair to deny your child the same right?

23. Don't

Don't be a tentative parent.

Why not?

All children need strong, constant guidelines while growing up. Sometimes, adoptive parents look upon themselves as not true parents, and unfortunately take a weaker, tentative approach to their child. This insecurity can also be compensated for by becoming too overbearing and controlling.

The adoptive parent has just as much right to parent as the biological parent. Values and standards need to be established and adhered to. All children need strong perimeters for behavior in order to feel safe. Adoptive parents need not second guess what biological parents (or other parents the child may have had) might do in a similar instance.

---

24. Do

Accept and understand your child's potential problem with trust.

Why?

He couldn't trust his own birth parents to keep him, why should he trust anyone else? When the all powerful parent/child relationship is broken, it is understandable how an adoptee can mistrust further relationships. In his mind he is thinking, "If my own mother gave me up, how can I feel safe that any relationship will last."

This can have implications within the adoptive family dynamics, as well as future dating or marriage relationships. Some adoptees feel this insecurity their whole lives.

Parents need to work overtime to reinstate the trust factor. Their child needs to learn he can always rely on his family. They can be trusted to love him always.

---

25. Do

Make it clear through words and actions that both adoptive parents wanted to adopt him.

Why?

Some adopted children grow up with the feeling that one of his parents was opposed to his adoption. When one parent is more dominant in the interaction with the child, he can sense (rightly or wrongly) that the other parent really didn't want him. This can happen particularly when business takes one parent away from home, and then whenever home, that parent doesn't interact very much with the child.

Remember, children can be egocentric. We must deal with their issues even when they are not rational to us as adults.

---

26. Do

Have sensibly high expectations for your child.

Why?

Some adopted children sense their adoptive parents don't have high expectations for them because they might have come from a questionable background. If children feel their birth parents didn't accomplish much in life, they can think their adoptive parents put them in the same category, and don't expect much from them. This can be damaging to the potential the child may have.

The child needs to be told he is master of his own destiny. He may feel doomed to follow in his birth parents' footsteps (and feel they are negative if they couldn't take care of a baby). High expectations and encouragement can go a long way here.

---

27. Do

Be human. Realize you don't have to be a perfect parent.

Why?

Your child needs to know he can be himself. He needs your example to know he should do his best, and though he may make mistakes, should keep trying to be the best person he can be.

INDEX